Praise for Fearless l

Today's tumultuous world requires extraordi political, military, business and not for pr it with the duality of emotional intelligence ...pred with courageous leadership, both are necessary. The book is chock full of very practical advice for leaders backed up by her years of experience working with leaders across all these sectors. A must read for those who want to not only build successful organizations today but build the leadership talent for tomorrows' organizations.

Noel Tichy, author of SUCCESSION: Mastering The Make-Or-Break Process of Leadership Transition; and Professor, The University of Michigan.

Fearless Leaders grabbed hold of me and wouldn't let go. It's the most practical book I've read on how to heighten mindfulness and ignite personal courage. It's a powerful book, tough at times, tender at others. From their own fearless experiences, and those of leaders they've studied, Cathy Greenberg and TC North offer revealing self-assessments, intimate first-person examples, and engaging applied exercises. Follow the steps outlined and they will enable you to achieve higher levels of performance and greater awareness of yourself and your environment. With Fearless Leaders as your guide you'll make better decisions and lead a more passionate life. You can't ask for more than that from any book!

Jim Kouzes-Author of The Leadership Challenge®

After having the pleasure of recording an On Demand Seminar with Cathy, I was astonished by Dr. Cathy Greenberg and TC North's ground-breaking perspective leadership, and the role Dr. Cathy takes herself as an inspirational leader. Not only did I learn to sharpen my focus, she also showed me how to achieve greater confidence and courage to become an inspirational leader myself. She was truly a pleasure to work with, and I am thrilled that she accepted to be a faculty at the Gazelles Growth Institute.

Daniel Marcos Gazelles Growth Institute- CEO

Cathy Greenberg and TC North's Fearless Leaders enlightens, inspires and provides the techniques to be an extraordinary leader. The mindfulness section is brilliant! I particularly liked the Creating Mindful Moments and Climbing the Consciousness Mountain chapters!

Jeremy Bloom-Three-time world champion freestyle skier; Co-Founder & President Integrate

Using stories that put faces on our fears and exercises to encourage self-discovery, Drs. Cathy Greenberg and TC North take us on a journey to first uncover our fears and then transform them. Fearless Leaders is not only for those who lead others; it is equally powerful for leading oneself through a fulfilling life.

Marian Head- Author of Revolutionary Agreements: Twelve Ways to Transform Stress and Struggle Into Freedom and Joy

Fearless Leaders provides techniques that can be used for any leader who wants to sharpen their focus—no matter who you are, where you are, or what your ultimate goals may be.

Gary Burnison-Award-winning author of "LEAD" and CEO of Korn Ferry International

We experienced the Fearless Leaders program first hand and learned more about our team in a day than we could have imagined with inspiring takeaways, more courage and motivated to focus on our mission to make every customer feel "fabulous" about their experience with us every day.

Jeff Warnick- Founder-Fabulous Freddy's

We invited Dr. Cathy Greenberg, author along with TC North of Fearless Leaders, and some of her colleagues to speak to an audience of high-level business professionals - and they were extremely impressed. They felt that the presentation added immense value to their working lives and gave them a new set of leadership tools and skills that they were previously unaware of. One of our audience members noted that the presentation was on the "celebrity" level - meaning that the content was so engaging and interesting that it felt like a unique, once-in-a-career opportunity. We are so thrilled to have had Cathy speak to our membership and we know that people took away of a lot of practical and important information.

Katrina Sawyer, Ph.D.- Assistant Professor of Psychology Graduate Programs in Human Resource Development Villanova University

Dr. Cathy Greenberg is a beautiful person who truly cares about making a positive difference. If you're ready to become a dynamic leader, then read, absorb and use the strategies in this brilliant book by Dr. Cathy Greenberg and TC North! Every leader should read this book!

James Malinchak "Founder, www.BigMoneySpeaker.com, Featured on ABCs Hit TV Show "Secret Millionaire"

Fearless Leaders by Dr. Cathy Greenberg and TC North shares our passion for developing world class leaders. At The Honor Foundation, based out of the Rady School of Management, our mission is to develop and transition the unique talents and skill sets belonging to our nation's most elite Special Operations Forces into the private sector of business. Fearless Leaders resonates with our unique community like we've never seen. Greenberg and North are molding our nation's warrior professionals into a new elite executive.

Joe Musselman, CEO - The Honor Foundation

Dr. Cathy Greenberg and TC North write about a subject near and dear to my heart: leadership. While leadership has always been the sine qua non of the military profession, it is becoming more recognized in law enforcement and is now entering the mainstream. Complex policy manuals, rigid command structures and stifling bureaucracies hold little attraction for a workforce used to obtaining what they want, when they want it and, in fact, operate as barriers to success. The authors begin with a very potent one-two punch with the first being fear. They show us rather than outside forces contradicting opportunity, it is our own fears that hold us back and prevent even an attempt to excel beyond the norm. In Fearless Leaders, Greenberg and North present fear as a very powerful paralytic foreclosing that which could be ours. The second topic is failure and, by way of example, they assure the reader even the most successful leaders fail. "Failure happens" may well be the next buzz phrase; the authors present failure as on opportunity to pause, assess, adjust and then begin moving forward again with resolve. "I'm scared"; check, everybody is. "I may fail"; check, probably so to some extent. Now move forward. With these two limiting factors addressed and out of the way, Greenberg and North have neutralized the two main obstacles to success and can begin their discussion of leading. They're on to something here; and I found the first chapter to be easily read, on point and a good starting point on the path to becoming a Fearless Leader.

Capt. Jay O. Coons, Ph.D. (HCSO), Criminal Warrants Division, Criminal Investigation Bureau

There is always room to learn more about leadership. Fearless Leaders guides the reader through a series of exercises, a mental audit if you will, that exposes your leadership mindset. Written in a self-directed style, the authors lead the reader on an introspective review of what fearless leadership is and how it can be developed. The principles provided are as applicable to law enforcement endeavors as well as to civilian enterprises.

Captain Kevan J. Dugan- Pennsylvania State Police (Ret.) - Former Director of Tactical Operations, BESO

An inspiring read in learning how to identify and master your fears. Dr. Cathy Greenberg and TC North present a useful, descriptive guide to accomplishing becoming a fearless leader. The book provides some great framework on how to do this, accompanied with some excellent examples and the integration of proven analysis and diagnosis that will no doubt help the reader to become a better fearless leader.

Luke Sherman - National Tactical Officer's Association - Central Region Director

Dr. Cathy Greenberg and TC North bring a level of excitement to their work that few professional coaches have, an ability to see past the present. They create an environment where your potential for success is just a natural extension of your talent and the added benefit of engaging your happiness and your fearlessness.

Johanna Dillon – Leadership Development, Cancer Treatment Centers of America

Dr. Cathy Greenberg and TC North are a true inspiration to others & great teachers on all aspects of coaching. I highly recommend Dr. Cathy Greenberg and TC North's approach on Leadership Training, & Coaching Programs for all ages. They are the best I have ever seen in the industry.

David Martin – Life Coach / Featured on America's Got Talent

Thank you Dr. Cathy Greenberg and TC North for investing in our organization. I really enjoyed your message and your Fearless Leader's model is something I think leaders can use to increase their effectiveness. You are creating a strong group of followers.

Bob Bortz - Manager - Learning & Talent Management , Global Fortune 500 Transportation Company

"Fearless Leaders" presents a captivating means of understanding and remembering critical mindset skills that can be applied to anything in life. The authors, Dr. Cathy Greenberg and TC North, encapsulate ideas that every person should study, no matter what their situation. Through examination of real life examples and simple, yet extremely useful tools, it provides thought provoking analysis of not only how to make us all better leaders, but better people. It should be mandatory reading for all.

Don Kester - Law Enforcement Executive and Trainer

"Fearless Leaders" paradoxically compels the reader to embrace failure. Dr. Cathy Greenberg and TC North masterfully position failure into a framework no professional should ignore.

Jim Whalen - Sheriff, Teton County, Wyoming

"If you aspire to be a great leader, one way or another you'll have to deal with your fear factor. I recommend you read Fearless Leaders to learn how other successful leaders have passed their fear thresholds. Don't be afraid, just read it and succeed."

Steven J. Stein, Ph.D. - CEO of Multi-Health Systems and co-author of The EQ Edge: Emotional Intelligence and Your Success

"Every successful leader needs to be fearless and this book walks you through the steps in such a simple, easy to implement way. It's renewed my sense of fearlessness!"

Kim Martin - Advisor to CEO of AMC Networks, Former President of WEtv

"Dr. Cathy Greenberg and TC North's methods are cutting-edge and based on scientific research of some of the most forward-thinking, relentlessly-fearless people alive today. With that said, if you don't read this book and begin to implement what applies to you, immediately, then you will be stopping yourself just short of reaching the true summit of success."

Chris Warner - Actor/Writer/Filmmaker/Speaker - Bringin' Badass Back to Hollywood

"Sponsoring the Fearless Leaders program at the Convenience Retail University provided an opportunity to gain valuable insight into the critical role that a positive mindset has on both our passion for success while acting with inspiring courage and how thinking from a higher consciousness can create a powerful focus on delivering outstanding customer service every day. Fearless Leaders was very motivating, I would highly recommend the Fearless Leaders program.

Steve Bradley - Corporate Vice President of Sales at Curtis Coffee Inc.

FEARLESS LEADERS

FEARLESS LEADERS

Sharpen Your Focus:
How the New Science of Mindfulness
Can Help You Reclaim Your Confidence

CATHY GREENBERG, PH.D.
AND
TC NORTH, PH.D.

Waterfront Digital Press

TABLE OF CONTENTS

ACKNOWLEDGMENTS

Cathy Greenberg, Ph.D.

I have worked in the military community for over a decade. Most recently with a rare breed of outstanding professional special forces operators who adhere to the ethos of the quiet professional as a trusted advisor.

In keeping with my work as a professional coach and trainer inside this highly calibrated community, it is my job to respect, protect and behave responsibly with anything utilized in the course of my ongoing capacity. As such, we will only use stories and names of members of the force that are already in the public domain and readily available to the private sector. I want to thank the entire community at the Naval Special Warfare Command and the U.S. Army for allowing me the honor of serving our mission to strengthen our leadership across the force and for your dedication to the resilience and readiness of our people, our soldiers and our nation. God bless you all and your families for all you do to contribute every day to building Fearless Leaders throughout your communities and on the battlefield.

In addition to these working warriors, I want to thank my own working warrior, Deputy Timothy J. Bingham, who was a first responder at the shooting of Gabrielle Gifford's (which spurred my deep interest in the subject of "Fearless Leaders")—just loving him, in addition to the privilege it has been to work among many other working warriors of his kind and to see them run towards danger into harms way in service to others, humbles me everyday. My lovely daughter Elisabeth, for her courage to fight for her own independence as a young, successful entrepreneur, in spite of health issues and other set backs, she has reclaimed her confidence and I love her "Fearless Leader" attitude. I will give TC, my co-author, the opportunity to share our gratitude and appreciation for the many wonderful "fearless, happy people" who supported, advised and contributed to the success of this endeavor. In addition to those in TC's acknowledgment that follows, I would also like to thank Marshall Goldsmith, Noel Tichy, Martin Seligman, Daniel Goleman, Mirabai Bush, Jim Kouzes, Mike Drew, Andrea Rendl, John Crosby, Relly Nadler, Steve Lanza, George Wright, Joe Theismann and James Malenchak. Many more names of those who made significant contributions to my thinking in particuler are named within these pages. Last but not least, gratitude to my fearless brothers, Fred and Phillip, for showing me what being courageous truly means everyday. As I like to say – Big

ACKNOWLEDGMENTS

TC North, Ph.D.

M astering fear and increasing courage, confidence and becoming more mindful is a lifelong journey.

The *Fearless Leaders* book is the result of learning from thousands of my clients, teachers and mentors. I'm so grateful for the experiences they have all shared with me.

I am also grateful for the guidance our literary agent, Bill Gladstone, who has great wisdom, and for the wonderful assistance with the manuscript by Summer Felix and Kenneth Kales, as well as for the collaboration with Cathy Greenberg to blend our experience and knowledge in the hope of creating more courageous, mindful and passionate leaders globally.

Several amazing people, true Fearless Leaders, allowed me during interviews to go deep inside their thinking to understand their secrets of success. These include Jeremy Bloom, Karl Mecklenburg, Rebecca Lolosoli and Alvaro Solano Delgado. Each of these individuals are not only incredibly successful, but they continue to improve our world through devoted service in their own ways.

I would also like to acknowledge my dad who recently passed; he was my first writing teacher. Being dyslexic, I always struggled with every aspect of the English language. Despite him being a journalism professor at a university, he still always believed in my writing ability. One of the chapters in this book is entitled, "The Impossible Is Possible." My becoming a writer probably fits that description.

I dedicate this book to the person I love the most in this world, my daughter Chelsea.

FOREWORD

Marshall Goldsmith

What does it mean to be fearless? According to Cathy Greenberg, Ph.D. and TC North, Ph.D., it means that you have a great deal of inspiring courage as a leader. In fact you have enough courage to fail and as a result you will succeed. In the authors' terms, it is put as such: "The courage to fail in order to succeed is the most ubiquitous success secret of Fearless Leaders, and it's also one of the characteristics that separate high performers from everyone else."

Fearless Leaders will help you understand this practically counter-intuitive axiom. It will give you the tools to practice it (and the other success secrets presented in this book) and it will help you help others become Fearless Leaders.

Cathy Greenberg and I have been friends and colleagues for more than 20 years. I am a great fan of her work. Cathy has not just the knowledge on this subject. She has not just done the research to understand fear. Cathy has experienced it and as you'll read in her story, she has mastered her fears. Like so many of us, life has dealt her a hand with which she could have crumbled. Instead, she has turned difficulties into success. As she says herself, "I needed to put my oxygen mask on first to save my daughter." In other words, she needed to master her fears in order to help others.

TC North's fear story is one to which many people can relate. In fact speech anxiety is one of the most common fears people have. Overcoming it, overcoming the ultimate fear of failure (that he would die during the presentation!) was a defining moment in his life.

Reading this book can be a defining moment in your life as you follow TC and Cathy through these pages as they explore and share the tools of mastering fear and explain the science of mindfulness. Techniques you'll learn, for instance, are The Four-Steps to Fear Mastery: 1) how to identify your fear; 2) how to embrace your fear and disempower it; 3) how to let go of your fear; 4) how to be free of fear.

With exercises and practical hands-on tips, *Fearless Leaders* provides all you will need to overcome your fear and be a success. Read it, enjoy it and learn from Cathy and TC about how to face, embrace and master your fears and turn them into success!

Marshall Goldsmith is the bestselling author or editor of 34 books, including the *New York Times* bestsellers, *MOJO* and *What Got You Here Won't Get You There.*

PREFACE

Steve Bonner

Welcome to the concept of "Fearless Leaders," a complex and nuanced concept well worth exploration with Cathy and TC. Once you consciously understand, harness and embrace fear, it will become a tool you will use to accelerate your journey of leadership, innovation and collaboration.

Everyone has experienced the reality of fear, and I suspect that as a leader you have sensed the advantages of fear, as well as its risks. As aspiring world class leaders, we are always a work in progress.

In the world today, only continuous change will achieve the potential we aspire to for our organizations and the people who look to us to lead. Change in turn implies moving out of our comfort zones and into the unknown. Fear lurks in that innovation, and as suggested, if we understand and can harness fear it will enhance the preparation for, execution of and success with change.

Fearlessness will also emerge from the inevitable failure that goes hand in hand with true innovation. None of us leads perfect innovation. In advance of innovation, well directed fear will help prepare us for the change; and when we do fail, fear will encourage us to study, learn, adjust and prepare for the next innovation.

Thus the concept of "Fearless Leaders" is a bit of an oxymoron. It seems a bit like our quest to extract simplicity from all the complexity in the world around us. Often the best we can do is to simulate simplicity…but that serves well most of the time.

In the same vein we will present and lead fearlessly…but only because we use fear so adeptly in our leadership roles. We will simulate fearlessness!

As CEO of Cancer Treatment Centers of America, I started in 1999 with a team of 300 innovators, and when I handed the reins to my successor last summer we had over 5,000 innovators. The company had grown to 22 times its size, with more capacity to change and improve than in 1999.

I never thought of fear as the tool Cathy and TC present here, but looking back, we shared lots of fear and broke new ground across the spectrum. We made mistakes; feared each one…but also tried to learn from each one, and more importantly used the fear of failure to better prepare for the next frontier.

I once studied with another innovator who taught us the process of mastery. We start as unconsciously incompetent with everything we learn…we do not know what we do not know. Then we progress to consciously incompetent…then we can become consciously competent and ultimately unconsciously competent. As we master our fears, we will use all the tools and advantages explained in this book…often times without even thinking about them.

Dr. Cathy Greenberg shared our innovation at CTCA—she was one of the board members at our western regional center in Arizona. Her relentless focus on the talent that drives our success added much to our progress, and *Fearless Leaders* will provide even more.

I hope you will turn the pages, and join the Fearless Leaders revolution. Lead on!!!

Steve Bonner is on the board of directors for the Cancer Treatment Centers of America.

INTRODUCTION

Have you ever wondered what goes through the mind of a world champion athlete in the final moments before they must compete? Jeremy Bloom, a three-time world champion freestyle skier describes with great candor exactly what he was thinking in the minutes before having to lay it all on the line at a world championship.

"A voice rang through the darkness of the starting area: 'Bloom on deck.' I shook out my legs; nervous energy filled my body. My muscles were tightening. I knew I had to stay loose. In about a minute, I'd be skiing for the freestyle world championship. I stretched my legs and swung my arms to loosen my chest and shoulders. While stretching my neck, I heard, 'Bloom in the hole.' I let my skis slide down closer to the starting gate, my heart raced and my breathing quickened. The guy before me took off and skied out of the darkness of the shadow of the starting gate and into the light of the mogul field. This is the moment I had worked years for… my mental training kicked in.

"I positioned my skis at the starting gate, focused on the first six inches of the course and thought: 'This is the single-most important turn. It's all I need to think about. Just make a good turn here, and my skills will carry me the rest of the way.' I imagined the perfect first turn.

"And then I built a barrier with my mind, a tunnel around the course that blocked everything out. It blocked out the TV cameras, the fans, my parents, everything and everyone. Now I existed inside my tunnel. All I could see, all that existed, was the course. My only thought was the first turn. The guy in front of me finished his run. My turn. I planted my right pole, then my left and then took a deep breath. Ready."

Bloom sounds almost superhuman in his ability to singularly focus on his goal while mentally blocking out all distractions along the way. But even more incredible, was he continued to use those very same techniques after retiring from skiing. After his skiing career, he went on to play three years of professional football in the National Football League and then built two successful businesses (during the Great Recession, no less), all by the age of 29.

What is his secret? How was he able to rise to the top of multiple fields at such a young age?

The answer will amaze you in its simplicity.

Bloom is a Fearless Leader.

What is a Fearless Leader?

A Fearless Leader is one who:

- *Acts with inspiring courage.*
- *Reacts with resilience.*
- *Thinks with mindfulness.*
- *Excels with unrelenting fire.*

All leaders—business, humanitarian, military or athletic—use the secrets and science of becoming Fearless Leaders. They continuously seek an edge to become great. We all have either conscious or subconscious fears that block our success. Fearless Leaders though take on and resolve their blocks to success by learning to master their fears. What's more, research we collected over a three-year period at national and global conferences with all female or all male audiences, as well as with mixed audiences, showed no difference in the capacity to be fearless or to act fearlessly. Additionally, our research applying both qualitative and quantitative interview techniques and methods across civilian, military or paramilitary professionals clearly demonstrated that both "working warriors" in the battlefield or in the boardroom were no more or less "capable of greater fearlessness" than the average individual.

Of the many thousands of leaders who have shaped history and changed the world, we'd like to acknowledge their contributions and share what we believe are their success secrets. Gandhi, the great Indian leader of the 20th century, was seen as a man of deep thought and wisdom. He had different ideas that were shunned by most. His methods of passive resistance, nonviolent disobedience, boycotts and hunger strikes influenced not only the British, who he sought his country's independence from, but impacted the entire world. His methods worked and so his messages carried on to other movements. Gandhi earned the title of Mahatma, "great soul," and encompassed all of the above characteristics of a Fearless Leader.

There are those who significantly shaped history like Abraham and Buddha, Catherine the Great and Genghis Khan. Queen Victoria and Nelson Mandela. Martin Luther King, Jr. and Charles Darwin. There are many more who have had a cultural impact and were influential in our evolution because they were, indeed, fearless.

What kind of impact could you have? How fearless are you? How fearless would you like to be? What if you had the right tools and guidance to accompany you on the journey? Would that make you feel more confident in your answers?

We certainly hope so, because that's exactly what we're here for. As high-performance executive and personal coaches we have become experts in combining the science of fearlessness with practical, strategic applications. It is our goal to help people in all walks of life develop a stronger mental game and increase the command they have over their personal and professional lives.

Inside this book are unique practices and habits, the secrets of success used by great leaders in various fields. They are the Fearless Leaders' secrets. All of the techniques outlined in these pages can be translated into use for any one—no matter who you are, what you do or what your ultimate goals may be. *Fearless Leaders* is your key to unlocking the knowledge, mindset and actionable techniques you need to become great. The best part is that you really only need to master one of the Fearless Leaders' secrets in this book to dramatically accelerate your abilities. If you are able to master just one success secret from this book you are extraordinary!

Fearless Leaders is a collection of real stories about real people, real experiences, real failures and real victories. We examine the science behind true fearlessness. We focus on emotional intelligence. We outline strategies and beliefs that clarify why it is so important that you be courageous, emotionally resilient and operate with mindfulness. These are all crucial factors in strengthening your mental and emotional muscles so that you can quickly adapt to change in an insecure world.

Few people will compete in a world championship like Jeremy Bloom. But that doesn't make it any less crucial for us to master the same skills he used to win. Personal strife, illness, financial loss and professional setbacks are common events that we all must face. No one chooses these, but you can choose how to respond to them.

In fact, we have both struggled with adversity, just like everyone else, and were able to come out the other side through the use of the very same techniques we write about here.

Cathy's Unforeseen Detour: Death and Divorce

By all outward indications, my life was a success. I had a lucrative career as an executive at a global firm. I was living in an eight-bedroom house on a large estate. My husband at the time was an executive at a large financial institution in New York. I had a beautiful, healthy daughter whom I adored. Any one would have looked at me and probably thought I didn't have a care in the world.

Although everything looked perfect from the outside, the reality was far from ideal. Between 1999 - 2002 I went through a very difficult separation and divorce and while it was not my choice to be single again, I wound up paying a large settlement in spite of the fact I was the single mother of a young child. I was totally taken by surprise when the court stipulated that. Because I was the major contributor to our household, I would have to bear the burden of making my former spouse whole during his pursuit of happiness. "REALLY, he wants out and I have to pay the price both emotionally and financially for something I was against? Don't I get a vote? I didn't want to be divorced, or alone or a single parent."

In the long run, I realized this was the price for being a successful global executive in a large and prestigious firm. As if that was not enough, during this time, both of my parents died in my arms; my dad passed as a result of a stroke on the eve of his 72nd birthday, Flag Day, and in the Jewish religion was buried soon after on Father's Day. My mom passed peacefully on her 68th birthday after a long battle with lung cancer and again was quickly laid to rest on Mother's Day. I remember thinking to myself, *did they really have to pass away on major holidays, as though I could forget them?* But it wasn't until I was diagnosed with two potentially terminal illnesses that I suddenly woke up and realized that *something was not right with my life.*

However, as a working mother, I didn't have the option of checking out when things felt overwhelmingly impossible. No matter how intense the pain, I still had to function. I needed to get up and out of bed each day so that I could pay the bills and care for my daughter. Even though I was surviving each day, if you peeled back the layers of my self-denial, you would have been shocked by the tremendous amount of grief and loss I was carrying deep within.

Eventually, my profound unhappiness began to ravage me physically, finding its way into my lymph nodes, my reproductive organs and almost destroying my immune system. Sometimes it got so bad that my entire body would go numb. It became abundantly clear that just focusing on the business of day-to-day survival was not enough to sustain a life. It was literally killing me.

I realized then that my happiness needed to come first, or there would be no one to take care of my young daughter and no job to support us. Just like they tell all parents before a plane takes off, in the event of an emergency you need to put your oxygen mask on first before you can save your child.

I needed to put my oxygen mask on first to save my daughter. Fortunately, around that time, my firm was going public with a stock offering (an IPO). My bosses knew just how miserable my life had become and came to me with great love and affection. They said, "You don't have to do this anymore if you don't want to."

So with my stock options, despite everything I had ever been told about having a backup plan in place when leaving a job, I took a yearlong break with no safety net. It was terrifying and exhilarating all at the same time. But that decision to gamble on myself led me on a journey to finding my life's work—opening the door for both men and women to find true happiness in their job and home. I was able to take much of my pain and suffering and apply it as a learning device to help other people going through detours in life. Knowing that I've been able to use my own difficult experiences to the benefit of others has been a great reward, second only to raising my beautiful daughter Elisabeth Oriana.

TC's Fork in the Road: A Defining Moment

Like most people, I've had challenges and setbacks throughout my life including growing up with alcoholic parents, being born with a leg deformity, being sexually molested, and due to a knee injury, losing the college athletic scholarship that would have financially allowed me to attend the university of my dreams.

I've also had defining moments when I had the choice between two very distinct paths to travel. For instance, I chose a road that has helped me rise above all the challenges I listed above. It happened when I was a 27-year-old working for Dr. Robert Swearingen at a wellness clinic as the exercise physiologist. One day, Robert asked, "Would you like to do a presentation on aerobic exercise for five to ten people at a local running store?"

Understand, I was a shy, introverted kid with dyslexia—I was the kid in grade school who didn't raise my hand for fear of being wrong. So my response to Robert's question was, "No! I don't do public speaking."

What happened next though changed my life forever. Robert, who towered over me, said in a very loud and authoritative voice, "Sit down."

With some trepidation, I sat.

"Do you want to be tops in your field?"

"Yes," I answered meekly.

Robert continued, "My advice, if you want to be your best, is that you learn to speak and write professionally and become good at them both. So accept this speaking engagement, accept every other speaking engagement that is ever offered to you and then create some more."

As terror gripped my body, I heard this voice in my head screaming *NO! NO! DON'T DO IT! RUN NOW!* I located the door with my eyes and began planning my exit. But there was this other tiny, quiet voice in my solar plexus, my intuitive voice that said, *he's right.* I had a choice, would I continue to use the excuse of being shy, introverted and dyslexic, or would I find the courage to do what it takes to become a leader in my field?

I decided to accept that speaking engagement and it took all the courage I had to just show up. I'd written my presentation on a pad of paper. I couldn't stand because my legs were shaking, so I sat in a chair. In front of my audience of six people, I read my whole presentation, word for word, off that pad of paper. I have to admit, it was a horrible presentation.

When it was over, I got in my car and collapsed into the front seat, completely drained of energy. Then, as I reflected on what I had just done, I suddenly thrust my hands into the air above my head and yelled, *"YES! THAT WAS GLORIOUS!"* I was ecstatic!

Why was I ecstatic? Because I hadn't died. Leading up to the presentation, my irrational fear was *if I present, I'll die.* Fear of death is the ultimate fear of failure.

I now am passionate about speaking and writing (as well as coaching) to empower people and build leaders globally. I have spent a lifetime learning to be courageous and bouncing back from more setbacks than I can even recall.

⚜ ⚜ ⚜

Science of Mindfulness

What is the science of mindfulness? We have studied the related body of knowledge and hope that you will benefit from what we discovered. To start off, here are the basics:

1. Our lives are healthier and can be better lived as an ongoing integration of our daily experience when we accept without judgement something that just is—such as discomfort, stress or unhappiness—and we choose to refocus our "energy" based upon the situations that present themselves to us as measured by time; hour by hour, day by day and week by week.
2. These "nonjudgmental" experiences help us create a momentary balance under great pressure, stress, fear or other states of a loss of joy.
3. When we engage in mindfulness we can still suspend the less than positive feelings and be joyful in the moment.

Why is the science of mindfulness so important to our individual collective consciousness? Because the innovative science of mindfulness takes you to a new level of potential for performance by focusing on being in the present, totally in balance with your skills, talents and life experiences. But, most importantly, when being mindful, you are without judgment, your focus and attention are sharpened, your mood is elevated and your overall life satisfaction is enhanced.

SECTION I: INSPIRING COURAGE

CHAPTER ONE
HAVE THE COURAGE
TO FAIL IN ORDER TO SUCCEED

"It is hard to fail, but it is worse never to have tried to succeed."
-Theodore Roosevelt

Does fear control you, or do you control fear? Do you have the courage to fail in order to succeed? Fearless Leaders don't like to fail. Some even say they hate to fail but, paradoxically, they learn to accept failure as an inevitable part of success. It turns out that the most enlightened people actually view their failures as mere setbacks and as opportunities to dissect, understand and learn from.

Achieving success requires failure—sometimes lots of it. Would you continue doing your job if you could be seriously injured or die a painful death from it? If you are willing to accept that physical risk, would you also be able to accept the emotional and psychological risks of failing in front of other people? These are the challenges that many Fearless Leaders accept. **The courage to fail in order to succeed is the first Fearless Leaders' success secret.**

We define the term "fearless" as one who masters his or her fears. By mastery we mean you still have fears but you are in conscious control of them. Fearless Leaders have especially learned to master the fear of failure and to use their setbacks as stepping stones for success. Not all Fearless Leaders share every one of the success secrets described in this book, but they all share this one. The courage to fail in order to succeed is one of the characteristics that separate high performers from everyone else.

Having the courage to fail is the opposite of being afraid to fail. If it's not managed and controlled, being afraid to fail blocks success. At a minimum, it can create anxiety. At its worst, it can emotionally paralyze you. Becoming great requires failure. To excel at being a Fearless Leader you must master coping with failure. Because the road to success is paved with the potholes of failure.

One of *Fortune's* Most Powerful Women in 2011, Susan Lyne, is a perfect example of a Fearless Leader willing to take risks and possibly fail in order to succeed. As a programming executive at ABC Entertainment, she wanted to steer away from the more male-dominated themes such as police shows and focus on more female-driven entertainment. The immense risks she took by championing shows for women like *Grey's Anatomy* and *Desperate Housewives* made the network extraordinarily successful.

Never one to shy away from controversy, Lyne was also instrumental in supporting the launch of *Lost,* which at the time, was considered to be a huge gamble. The show went on to be a ratings mega-hit for six seasons and won countless awards, including a Primetime Emmy for Outstanding Drama Series in 2005 and 2006.

But not even those enormous successes could insulate Lyne from professional failure. Much to her surprise, she was fired from ABC in 2004. This was a huge setback for her. But Lyne is an exemplary Fearless Leader in that even after being fired and experiencing a catastrophic career failure, she continued to be courageous and move on. Within one year of losing her job at ABC, Lyne joined Martha Stewart Living Omni Media as the CEO where she was enormously effective in inspiring and encouraging the people around her to excel.

Lyne is a risk taker who has faced the possibility of failure many times on her journey to success. She said, "I've taken a leap of faith on several occasions, and in every case, on some level, I've become a beginner again."

By refusing to stay with what's familiar in her career, and by being courageous enough to take on enormous new challenges, Lyne has risen to the top time and time again. She embodies many of the qualities of a Fearless Leader with her ability to act with inspiring courage, react with resilience and excel with unrelenting passion.

Stepping off the path of familiarity into the unknown is common to other successful individuals as well. In fact, the ability to take a leap of faith is a characteristic of success. Certainly, when Christie Hefner became president of the then financially ailing Playboy Enterprises, it took nerves of titanium just to take on the role. But then she showed even more courage in admitting that some things just weren't working. She disposed of the clubs, the modeling agency and the book division and pushed the company into the nascent area of cable television. She engendered success by daring to take something big and scaling it back.

In our interview with Christie, she stated, "Life is a trapeze act. It's a series of opportunities presented and taken. You have to *seem* available to actually get the opportunity." Throughout her life, she would have loved to have had more opportunities, but because people saw her as the leader of the Playboy brand, they assumed she wasn't available. She said that no one sets out on a course to fail and that it's really about the risk / reward proposition that is much more meaningful and manageable in one's life.

She also shared a poignant but meaningful exchange with her father, Hugh Hefner. He was at one point fearful that Christie might take Playboy in a direction that truly could have ended his lifetime achievement. "Whatever you do Christie, don't sell the mansion." Christie, unstoppable in her passion for success took his plea with good humor and forged ahead.

She demonstrated her ability and determination to take risks again in 2008, choosing to strike off in a different direction when she ended her 20-year association with the company her father had founded. She said that after she left Playboy, the wonderful opportunities she had hoped to find were indeed coming at her fast. Her ability to be resilient and to find different approaches to her life brought about changes including redefining her focus. The end result is that she is living a happy life and loving what she is doing.

Are the Best in the World Afraid of Failing?

Jeremy Bloom, the three-time world champion freestyle skier, former NFL player and now successful entrepreneur, who we wrote about in this book's introduction, was asked in our interview, "Have you ever failed?"

"Oh, I've failed much more in my life than I've succeeded," he answered. "Much more. I don't look at them as failures though. I look at them as setbacks, and I love setbacks because I think every setback gives you an opportunity to separate from everyone else."

From Bloom's perspective, setbacks identify the most challenging situations to solve and he recognizes those are the opportunities that most people won't, or can't, solve. Thus, if he and his team can solve them, they will experience breakthroughs that separate them from the competition.

Six-time All-Pro NFL linebacker and former team captain for the Denver Broncos, Karl Mecklenburg, explains, "In the NFL you see gifted guys who were drafted in the first or second round, but the first time they have ever failed was on their first day at an NFL training camp when some veteran mops the floor with them. They don't know how to react. They feel defeated. On the other hand, if you have someone who has been thwarted and challenged, and has pushed himself over and over again up to that line where they *are* going to fail, but have the courage to continue, that is someone who can handle failure. They're the football players who make it in the pros."

Mecklenburg used setbacks from earlier in his life, like losing his college football scholarship, as learning opportunities. His motivation to succeed became intense because of his setbacks. As you read the secrets in this book, you will notice that not only did Mecklenburg demonstrate inspiring courage through his willingness to fail in order to succeed, but also great resilience and passion.

Rebecca Lolosoli, who lives in Kenya and is part of the Samburu tribe, is another example of a Fearless Leader who inspires others with her courage. In her culture, women are considered possessions. They can be bought and sold for less money than the price of a cow. She explains: "A husband is expected to beat his wife so that [she doesn't] 'grow horns'"—which really means to make sure she doesn't think and act independently. "A husband may even kill his wife without being punished."

Even as a girl, Lolosoli would intervene when a woman was being attacked while knowing she herself would be punished for her rescue efforts. She often stood up in front of the village elders, asking that they put an end to the violent customs against females, like mutilating girl's genitalia. She would also provide protection to those who were outcasted because they had been raped. Despite the horrific, cruel treatment inflicted on her, she endured. Lolosoli was fearless and continued to speak out against the abuse of women.

As an adult, she received death threats from her husband and men in the area. Once, her husband's brothers beat her so badly that she was blinded for nearly two months. But as soon as she recovered, Lolosoli continued fighting for the empowerment of the women in Kenya by forming a new village, a safe haven for females fleeing violence or persecution. They named it Umoja, which means unity. Lolosoli continually demonstrates the courage to fail, or in her situation the courage to risk rape, physical beatings and death, in order to succeed at empowering women.

The Wisdom of Learning from Failure

In an article in the *Harvard Business Review*, Amy Edmondson observes: "We are programmed at an early age to think failure is bad. That belief prevents organizations from effectively learning from their missteps." But this presents a paradox. How do organizations create an environment in which people can freely admit to failures, avoid blame and react constructively to those failures while not succumbing to an "anything goes" mentality? As she points out, "the slogan 'fail often in order to succeed sooner' would hardly promote success in a manufacturing plant."

How to learn from failure? Edmondson suggests three remedies: reduce the stigma of failure by avoiding the "Blame Game," thoroughly analyze the causes of that failure and then dig in and discover the wisdom gained from it, and actually produce failure through systematic experimentation to better learn from it.

In another article, Edmondson says that in what is increasingly a knowledge economy, "even flawless execution cannot guarantee enduring success." Instead, people must encourage new ideas and experimentation with those ideas, risking failures today that can bring greater success tomorrow.

To strengthen your courage to fail in order to succeed, there are three important parts for you to address:

Define what success is for you.
Learn to strengthen your courage.
Become a master of your fear of failure.

Exercise: Define What Success is For You

- What is personal success?

  _____

  _____

  _____

  _____

- What is success in your professional life? Do you know why you define success this way?

  _____

  _____

  _____

  _____

- What do you want to be most proud of?

  _____

  _____

  _____

  _____

Learn to Strengthen Your Courage

Technique 1 - Instant Access to Courage

Your memories are all linked in your brain by neurons; these linked neurons are called a neural network. Essentially, all of your courageous memories are also linked together in their own neural network. So when you think from your courageous neural network you will experience more courage in your mind, body and emotions. It's analogous to using a computer. If your brain is your computer, it contains all of your applications and you can choose which ones you want to use. Your courageous neural network is in essence your courageous application. To open this application all you need to do is access a memory of a time when you showed courage. When you do this, your courageous app opens.

Here though is an important way a neural network is different from a computer application. Each time you think about an experience in which you were brave, you stimulate and strengthen your courageous neural network. Just like muscles in your body, neurons and neural networks in your brain can literally become bigger and stronger as you exercise (stimulate) them.

Technique 2 - Stimulating Your Courageous Neural Network

Remember. Think of a time when you were brave. It could be from your childhood, teenage years or adult life. It could involve academics, a social activity, a game, athletics, a hobby or a time when you were scared.

Feel the courage. Continue recalling as much detail as possible until you can begin to re-experience some of the bravery you had when this event actually occurred. You will likely notice feeling more courageous as you immerse yourself in this memory. Through this, you will learn to program your mind to have more inspiration for the events you will need courage for in your future.

Become a Master of Your Fear of Failure

Don't let fear destroy your dreams. Fear of failure is a common block to success. It exists at both the conscious and subconscious levels of your mind. If fear of failure, either consciously or subconsciously, controls your thoughts and decision-making, the possibility of your obtaining the success you seek is slim. To become a Fearless Leader, you must gain control of and eventually master the fear of failure.

Notice we use the term "master" fear of failure, not "purge" or "eliminate" fear of failure. We want you to have a healthy awareness of your fear of failure, use it as a warning, which is it's purpose, and learn to control it so it's not in control of you. Fear, from an evolutionary perspective, is a survival adaptation that is useful in helping you recognize danger, so you, like all of us, will experience fear at times. You need to understand why you have a fear of failure in order to gain control of it.

The Nine Faces of Fear of Failure

The next part of this chapter will help you identify the nine faces of fear of failure, how to overcome them and accept the possibility of failure so you can focus your mind on successfully attaining your goals and dreams.

Fear of Failure Face #1: Not Giving 100 Percent

This fear comes from the belief that if you give 100 percent and fail, then you're a failure. This is the most devastating form of fear of failure because it seems hopeless, as if you're permanently flawed. Correct this thinking by reframing your thoughts or changing your beliefs. A reframed thought for an entrepreneur could be: "I will give 100 percent to build my business. If it doesn't succeed, I'll take what I learn and either modify the business or start a different one with a greater chance to succeed."

Fear of Failure Face #2: Procrastination

When you're afraid to fail and you think you might, you put off doing things so you don't have to confront the consequences. An officer may procrastinate on implementing a new strategy or initiative because he is afraid it might fail. Or, an entrepreneur may put off firing an employee for fear that she will spend a lot of resources hiring someone new who may possibly be worse, so she continues with the known person.

As an example, a CEO of a high-tech firm of about 60 people had a sales team that was underperforming and was told by his board: "One of your weaknesses is that you wait too long to make personnel changes." When he realized this was true and embraced facing this fear of failure, it lost its power. After that, he made personnel changes quickly when they were needed.

Fear of Failure Face #3: Anger

Instead of dealing directly with your fear, you express it as anger or as rage, so no one sees the fear, possibly even yourself. There's a good chance you don't even know you have a fear of failure because it is quickly covered up by defensiveness. Expressing anger won't resolve the real issue when it's actually a fear of failure. In fact, expressing anger will probably only create a new set of problems. Anger can be deceptive and destructive because when the anger is expressed, sometimes being unleashed on a person or situation that has nothing to do with the original agitant, it can hurt relationships. Find the fear, then work to resolve it and your anger can disappear.

Fear of Failure Face #4: Crying

There are a variety of reasons people cry, including emotional pain, physical pain and grief. Crying is a fairly normal response to fear, including the fear of failure. Most young children cry openly when scared, but for adults to cry out of fear is considered something best done in private. Crying can be cathartic. However, if it's being used as a cover-up for fear, you need to deal directly with your feelings of being afraid.

Fear of Failure Face #5: Rationalizing

After losing a big deal, the sales rep says, "I didn't have much of a chance anyway." Don't deceive yourself or make excuses. What if you want a new job or a promotion; will you go all out for it? Or rationalize that you don't have a chance and either not go for it or give a half-hearted effort? You'll win some and lose some, but the only way to win big deals is to keep focused, play big and learn from winning and losing.

Fear of Failure Face #6: Avoidance

When you avoid putting yourself in situations where you think you could fail, you set yourself up for a life as an underachiever. Underachievers stay in their comfort zone. For them, confronting the possibility of failure is too uncomfortable, whereas high performers live and thrive with challenge and discomfort. The possibility of failure motivates high performers to take positive action. Take the first step in resolving this fear by identifying what you are avoiding. There are additional techniques to resolving this fear discussed later.

Fear of Failure #7: Indecision

A fairly common face of fear of failure is indecision. Indecision is a decision…the decision to not change anything now. It's an inaction that keeps things the same. Fearless Leaders are good decision makers. Sometimes the decision is to do nothing, but doing nothing is made as an active decision, not as a passive lack of action. When indecisive, consider making a conscious decision to either do nothing, or to take action.

Fear of Failure Face #8: "*Nexciting*"

Do you know someone who is always chasing a new, shiny ball— someone who's always after the newest "thing," be it a new idea, a better product or service—before finishing what has already been started? Chasing what's new and exciting ("nexciting") can keep someone energized even though he is not succeeding at much of anything. He's afraid of failure and covers this up with the drug of "nexciting." To help you overcome this, consider having strong, positive accountability to follow through on all that is important to you.

Fear of Failure Face #9: Withdrawal

A mild form of withdrawal would be similar to procrastination or avoidance. In an extreme case, you could be curled up in bed in the fetal position. If the fear is so big that it immobilizes you emotionally and you withdraw, you may not be ready for the challenge. Let it go or find someone to help you by either doing it together or assisting you to find the courage or skills you need to increase your confidence and probability for success. If your withdrawal is severe, consider the help of a mental health professional.

Technique - The Four-Step Mastery of Fear of Failure

These four simple, but powerful steps can help you master many of your fears, including the fear of failure:

Identify your fear. What are you afraid you'll fail at?

Embrace your fear. Gently embrace your fear; imagine it. What does it look like? What might it sound like? Does it have a name? Remember, you have created this fear and continue to create it, so you have developed this fear for a reason. Its original purpose was to protect you, but now it's holding you back.

Understand you are not your fear. Fear of failure is not you. Your fearful thoughts have created an emotion, but you're not your thoughts or your emotions. Use the image you created in the previous step to understand that your fear is not you.

Be free of fear. What would your life be like if you were in control of fear of failure? How would you sit, walk and move about? Can you imagine what it might feel like to confront the challenges that used to hold you back? Can you hear how you would speak if you were free of your fear? As you experience this, imagine focusing on being successful in attaining what you have been afraid to fail at. Focus on the thoughts, feelings and actions most associated with you being successful. Repeat this step over and over until you have mastered your fear.

The Biggest Misinterpretation of Failure

Most people don't like to fail and if you personalize failure—such as failing at a new business, job or marriage—it's really easy to misinterpret that failure as meaning, "I'm a failure" or "I'm a loser." But you're not!

When you do something that's important to you and it doesn't work out, it's a setback, not a failure. Embracing setbacks does not make you a failure and in fact your courage to do so can inspire others. If you mistakenly believe you're a failure when things don't work out as planned, then you will experience high degrees of fear when confronting risks.

Productive Paranoia

In the book *Great by Choice,* Bill Gates is described as having been hypervigilant about what could damage Microsoft. He said in 1994, "I consider failure on a regular basis...Fear should guide you." When your company is the leader in its field and one of the largest in the world, there are countless other organizations, individuals and circumstances that could bring you down. Gates understood this and confronted potential failure every day.

Productive paranoia is the ability to be hypervigilant about potentially bad events that can hit your company or you personally, and then turn that fear into preparation and clearheaded action. You can't sit around being fearful; you must act. Fear is a form of energy. Fearless Leaders use that energy to go into productive, focused action.

SHARPEN YOUR FOCUS

Throughout the book we're going to ask you to take some time to think about what you've learned and briefly summarize that knowledge in spaces like that below. When you've finished reading this book, these collected thoughts will provide you with a shot of "instant" inspiration as you apply these lessons to your life.

_____

_____

_____

_____

_____

Chapter Two
Get Comfortable Being Uncomfortable

"Life begins at the end of your comfort zone."
– Neale Donald Walsch, author

The second Fearless Leaders' success secret is **be comfortable being uncomfortable**. It's the discomfort that you may feel when you're being courageous; it's the nervousness you might have before a job interview; it's the pressure you could feel coming up against an important deadline; it's the butterflies you may feel in your stomach before a competition; it's the gut-check you might need before committing enormous resources to a new strategy. It happens to the humanitarian who knows she might be killed for speaking her truth and to the special forces operator who risks his life with every mission. And it happens to you when you take on a challenge and stretch your comfort zone.

Because of genetics or social development, or both, some people are risk-adverse while others enjoy risk. Fearless Leaders relish the excitement of the challenge. It's uncomfortable but still they are comfortable in it. In fact, they usually thrive in the discomfort of a good challenge.

If you master this Fearless Leaders' secret, it will help you create the mindset that it's good to be uncomfortable taking on a challenge. You will then take intelligent risks and learn and grow in both your business and personal lives. If you never master this success secret of getting comfortable being uncomfortable, you will likely stay in your comfort zone.

"I WILL NEVER QUIT."

That statement is not just a phrase on Captain Iván Castro's Army Special Forces insignia; it's both a statement of purpose and the philosophy by which he lives his life. *Tip of the Spear,* a magazine dedicated to supporting our special forces, tells the story of Captain Castro:

While fighting insurgents in a mud-walled compound in Iraq, a mortar hit the rooftop on which he was standing. The horrific wounds he suffered made it necessary for medics to check his dog tags to identify him. When he regained consciousness he was met by the darkness of irreversible blindness and a deep, lingering, utterly debilitating despair. Castro even wished that he had not escaped traumatic brain injury (TBI) reasoning that at least TBI would have blocked him from fully understanding how his life was changed forever.

All of this began to turn around though as he recognized that other soldiers who had experienced TBI were now unaware of their surroundings, and were much worse off than he was. When he met Mike Jernigan, a Marine veteran who had also lost his eyesight in service to his country, and realized the way in which he had rebuilt his life despite his blindness, Castro resolved to make his own life the best it could be. He chose to start by running in the next Marine Corps marathon.

Since that time, Castro has competed in the 2012 Warrior Games, ridden a bicycle across the country and taken part in numerous marathons. When asked why he continues in his exhausting efforts, he simply replies, "I will never quit."

Destructive and Constructive Anxiety

Excessive stress and anxiety can hurt you mentally, emotionally and physically. Excessive negative stress will actually block your use of the executive part of your brain, the most advanced portion where your willpower and higher consciousness thinking takes place. In sports and performance psychology, it's well known that there is a very specific relationship between performance (the vertical axis) and anxiety or stress (the horizontal axis) as shown in the diagram below.

Flow was originally described in the book *Flow: The Psychology of Optimal Experience* by Mihaly Csíkszentmihalyi.

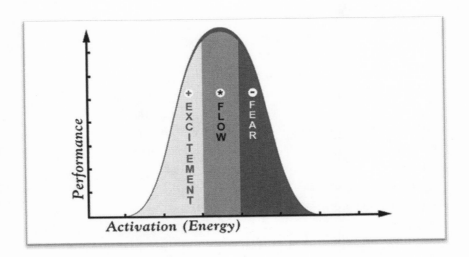

Being nervous or anxious are neither helpful nor hurtful, in and of themselves. However, using your discomfort to be in what experts often call "the zone" is a huge opportunity. When you're in the excitement part of the curve or peak performance zone, you are experiencing what is known in psychology as "challenge stress," which gears you up to be your best and compete well. This is different than what's on the right side of the curve, "threat stress," which will douse your enthusiasm and desire.

When you experience threat stress, you may not believe you can handle the situation and this can trigger the classic fight or flight response from the emotional center of the brain. Your perception of a given situation will determine whether you experience stress as excitement (challenge stress) or fear (threat stress).

Leadership Benefits of Being Uncomfortable

Do you inspire others with your courage and willingness to take well thought-out risks? Do you stay with what's comfortable or push yourself out of your comfort zone and inspire others to do the same?

Can you imagine an athlete who only trains in comfort and never pushes into discomfort or pain? An athlete has to train into discomfort and even into pain to become stronger, faster, better—so do you.

This concept was illustrated by Marty Seligman in a discussion with *The Blank Slate* author Steven Pinker. Seligman says that the period in which everyone regards things like sadness, anxiety and anger as problems that can be therapeutically and/or pharmaceutically eradicated has passed. According to him, therapists and patients should now adopt the concept that he calls "Dealing with It."

During a personal interview with Seligman on *Leadership Development News* (a top rated business talk radio show hosted by Drs. Cathy Greenberg and Relly Nadler on the Voice America Network), he refers to the way in which the armed services trains snipers. Because it frequently takes as long as 24 hours for a sniper to get into position and another 36 hours of staying motionless before they can get off their shot, sleepiness becomes a significant issue. A therapist would prescribe drugs to keep them awake or instruct them in techniques to overcome fatigue. Sniper trainers take a very different approach though, one that is closely aligned with Seligman's notion about just "Dealing with It." The concept of dealing with it is to practice and accept any pain and discomfort associated with the action or activity you are undertaking. If a sniper has to stay still for hours at a time in cold weather, then they practice staying still in cold weather so they can deal with it.

How successful do you think an entrepreneur would be if she didn't risk differentiating and innovating? Entrepreneurs must continually challenge the status quo. Thus, they live in discomfort. The best entrepreneurs thrive on being uncomfortable.

Feel Like a Fraud?

50, 150, 500? We can't even count the number of highly success-ful executives, entrepreneurs and sales professionals who've told us, "I feel like a fraud," or something similar—and all of these talented people had a secret fear. Like one businessman we'll call Dan:

Dan was tremendously successful and powerful in his city and speaking to groups was important for his stature. He used to enjoy speaking, but was becoming increasingly terrified of it. The greater his success, the more he felt like a fraud. And the more he felt like a fraud, the greater his fear of public speaking became. Dan's secret? He'd dropped out of school in the eighth grade, gotten a GED and never attended college. Now he was negotiating multimillion-dollar deals with some of the most brilliant business minds in the country. What if they found out he was an eighth-grade dropout? To over-come this fear, Dan decided on two courses of action.

First, Dan completely reframed his feeling from having a nega-tive charge (fear) to a positive charge (excitement). Here's how he did it. He was an adrenaline junkie who loved to rock climb, parachute and paraglide. Yet, public speaking scared him. So he was asked: "What if you thought about public speaking as the most amazing, exciting, adrenalin rush you've ever had, bigger than rock climbing or jumping out of a plane?"

After contemplating this reframed thought, he said, "When I think about it like that it's the greatest rush I could ever imagine!" And with that, he created a new belief which was, "Public speak-ing...what a rush!"

For his second course of action, Dan decided to reveal his secret in the business section of his city's newspaper. It was a story about an incredibly brave, tough and intelligent kid who survived at a young age on ghetto streets where many die. To get through, he studied and became a highly ranked karate fighter. And to thrive and later become an articulate, knowledgeable business owner, he became a voracious reader, educating himself through amazing desire and self-discipline. His published story created admiration for him throughout the community. He exposed everything in his article, and by doing so, freed himself from the fear of being found to be a fraud. His colleagues were amazed that he could be such an intelligent businessman without a college education.

Exercise: Your Secret Fears

- Do you have fears you keep secret? Have the courage to free yourself from your secret fears and gain more confidence. What is it you are afraid people will find out about you?

_____

_____

_____

_____

- What can you do to free yourself from your secrets?

_____

_____

_____

_____

Fearless Leaders often push themselves beyond what others would consider, and stay focused on their vision and long-term goals. This is an important aspect to getting comfortable being uncomfortable.

How Can You Get Comfortable with Being Uncomfortable?
Fearless Leaders are not devoid of fear; rather they are people who don't let fear destroy their dreams. They recognize that the inability to take risks in the face of fear can be more dangerous to them and to those around them than anything that can happen as a result of their actions.

Leymah Gbowee: Portrait of a Fearless Leader
The country of Liberia was ravaged by a tragic 14-year long civil war. During that time, one in three Liberians was displaced, and

hundreds of thousands of young girls, mothers and grandmothers were raped and murdered by soldiers on both sides of the conflict. Astonishingly, this horrific battle was ended not by the soldiers or the diplomats, but by a mother who didn't want her children, or any Liberian child, to have to grow up in a war zone.

Just 17 when the war began, Leymah Gbowee had to witness first-hand the terrible violence that had ripped families and loved ones apart for more than a decade. She was so devastated by what she saw that she no longer found comfort in prayer. Her faith was replaced with anger. Then one night, as she slept, Gbowee had a dream that told her to gather women and work for peace.

She initially resisted this calling because she really had no desire to lead. In her country, women were considered trouble. Also, it seemed like an insurmountable obstacle for the Liberian women to ever come together for any common good. But the voice within Gbowee would not be stilled. This was her country and these were her friends and her family living in a war zone and experiencing all the atrocities of war. So, she chose to own the war and find a way to end it.

With ten U.S. dollars and seven women, Gbowee formed the Christian Women Peace Initiative. Soon, Muslim women began their own group and eventually the two organizations joined together to form a partnership for peace.

Gbowee explained, "We used our pain, our broken bodies and scars to confront the terrors." These extraordinary women focused on the cause closest to their hearts—the children. They realized that the only way to ensure the survival of their young ones was to acknowledge and accept the humanity in their oppressors. The women understood that many of their rapists had been boys, as young as nine-years-old, who were kidnapped and forced to become soldiers in the conflict. The boys had grown into dangerous men with guns, but they were still wounded and broken.

How did Gbowee have the inspiration to lead such a noble resistance movement within her homeland? Faith gave Gbowee the courage to be a Fearless Leader. The government officials finally agreed to speak with her. She was only 31-years-old at the time and was instructed to be diplomatic. She was told what to say and what not to say. She was forbidden from challenging the political figures' authority.

But as she entered the government building, Gbowee realized that the only voice she needed to listen to was her own intuitive one. So in a bold move, fueled by her deep sense of integrity and courage, she stood up before the leaders of Liberia and demanded that they take action to stop the rapes and murders of innocent people. She demanded that they end the war.

Perhaps as a result, the warlords and government leaders began peace talks that continued for months. Each day Gbowee and her group of women, even while they were laughed at and criticized, waited outside the building where the negotiations were taking place.

Then, when the peace talks hit an impasse, Gbowee was crushed. She gave up protesting and all other actions until one day she happened to see a video that showed how a bomb had killed two young boys who had been brushing their teeth. All that was left of them were their slippers.

Gbowee went into immediate action. She gathered the women for peace together and alerted the press that something big was about to happen. What were her plans? The truth was she had none. Gbowee only knew that she had to do something, now.

She told the group of women to link hands, and together they headed to the government building. United, they blocked the door where the officials were about to exit. The women were informed that they had to leave or they would be arrested. That would mean rape, torture, humiliation and ultimately death.

But the women sat down and refused to move.

When security forces came, Gbowee said, "I'll make it easy for you. I'll strip naked. I am protesting the pain of every woman. Take what is left of womanhood for every Liberian woman. If this will bring peace then take it!"

It's important to understand that in some African cultures a woman publicly taking off her clothes is considered shameful. To the men who are witnesses, it is considered a curse. The other women next to Gbowee followed her lead and stripped as well. The security men ran away. And in that moment, that defining mindful moment, this group of women became a force to be reckoned with. After that, as Gbowee said, "We understood we, too, had power."

The peace talks resumed and three weeks later a lasting agreement was signed.

Gbowee's leadership and the women activists' inspiring courage and commitment was the catalyst for ending the Liberian civil war. Their actions exemplified the qualities that topple governments, transform nations and create miracles. These women were Fearless Leaders. Leymah Gbowee was awarded the Nobel Peace Prize in 2011 for her actions.

Apart from fear of death, or the fear of failure which we have already discussed in the first chapter, there are other fears that can also limit you. These include fear of success, fear of rejection and fear of selling. Which of these fears may have limited you?

Fear of Success

This is one of the most universal of all fears. It is more complicated than most people think, affecting politicians, sports stars and definitely mothers and fathers. The fear of success is caused by a conflict between goals; one goal that you are working hard to achieve and if accomplished, could make it difficult to attain one of your other important goals. Either consciously or unconsciously, you can sabotage your own success in accomplishing your first goal because you are afraid it will keep you from obtaining your other goal.

Here are examples of the fear of success:

The Young Entrepreneur

Sarah was a thirty-something entrepreneur who owned a small wealth management firm. She sought help to grow her business. When discussing what could be holding her back from greater success, she said, "I don't think my family will accept me if I'm wealthy because my parents always say wealthy people are evil." Sarah had a clear conflict between her desire to be personally wealthy and an equally strong desire to be loved by her family. She initially believed that she could only be successful at one or the other, but not both.

She resolved this with an imperfect but effective strategy by creating wealth but staying very humble and understated about it with her family. Sarah was thus able to become both wealthy and remain loved by her family.

Hundreds of Business Executives

Business executives are constantly concerned about achieving success in both their work and personal lives. Again, so many people see this as an either/or situation. But the resolution involves finding a way to be successful at work and with family. Don't ask yourself: "How can I be more balanced?" It's the wrong question. Highly successful people often don't always live a balanced life, but they can live a life that is successful in all respects.

Sheryl Sandberg, author of *Lean In: Women, Work and the Will to Lead*, has mentioned that one of her favorite posters states: "Done Is Better Than Perfect." What does this mean in terms of an integrated life? Sandberg says that embracing this motto requires one to "let go of unattainable standards," to recognize that you are not perfect and, whether you are at home with the family, out with friends or engrossed in your work, enjoy what you have at that particular moment in time.

Technique - Resolving the Fear of Success

Define one of your most important goals. Then search your mind for potential conflicting goals.

To help you identify competing goals, answer the following questions: If I attain this goal, what will change? Who will I spend time with? How will my self-image change?

Will changes in your life occur when and if you attain this goal? Will these be changes for better or for worse? If in this step you identify a change that you don't like and that may even make you unhappy, realize you are in control. You have the power to decide if this change will occur or not.

Fear of Rejection

Inherent to fear of rejection is the irrational belief that others will not accept you for who you are, what you believe and how you act. This fear blocks you from being your true self.

Fear of rejection will also cause you to procrastinate and not do many of the things that will improve your business and personal relationships. This will lead to irrational thinking and self-defeating behavior. Part of overcoming fear of rejection is to understand that you are a human being of good character and good ethics; you are fundamentally a good person.

TC and Hockey

I grew up playing hockey, which taught me a great lesson about rejection. In hockey, about 90 percent of all shots taken on goal are rejected (blocked by the goalie). However, as Wayne Gretzky, known as "The Great One" in hockey, is credited with saying, "100 percent of the shots you *don't* take don't go in." If you're discouraged by the nine out of ten shots that don't go in, and don't take any shots, in hockey, you'll never score.

Fear of Selling

Fear of selling is prevalent in both men and women and at all levels of success including Fortune 500 CEOs, small business owners, military leaders and humanitarians. There are many reasons for the fear of selling. As *Bloomberg Business Week* writer Michelle Nichols points out, you can be afraid of approaching a new customer, entering an unknown environment, being embarrassed or not having an answer to a question. Or perhaps you're concerned that a failure to sell will result in the end of your career. What you need to ask yourself though is "what's the worst thing that can happen if I try to sell this idea, product or myself?" Chances are, even if you lose the sale, your life will go on. Besides, you may even succeed!

As an entrepreneur, you not only lead the development of your company's vision and strategies, you also have to sell them to your entire team. You may not realize it, but you are selling ideas all of the time. You will be more influential, more successful and happier if you sell well.

A long-time client turned friend and highly respected executive in the insurance industry, Bill Lombardo, is a master training specialist and the winner of several major awards from the distinguished magazine, *CLO (Chief Learning Officer)*. Bill has been recognized nationally for his outstanding agent training programs including "Top Gun," a progressive emotional intelligence based process for increasing success in sales. He says, "It's easy to see how individual beliefs about sales capability can get in the way of young agents or more seasoned agents who have the challenge of new service offerings in a growing, wealth management environment. It's my goal to create scenario planning that enables a change in their beliefs that shifts their mindset to create the opportunities for increased performance and greater life satisfaction in all our agents."

How Do You Overcome a Fear of Selling?

Technique 1 - Focus on Serving

All your fears about selling are "me fears." Me failing, me being rejected, me looking foolish, me not knowing enough. Instead, get your focus off yourself; be completely focused on serving others.

Technique 2 - Resolving Fear Using the Worst-Case Scenario

This fear-busting technique can be extraordinarily powerful, not only for fear of rejection, but also for almost all fears. When you can accept the worst case, you no longer need to fear it, and you can focus on what you want and go after it:

Describe it. Describe in great detail the worst-case scenario.

How probable is it? How probable is it that this worst case will come true? It's sometimes useful to use a zero to 100 percent scale where zero is no possibility and 100 percent is it's certain it will happen. Answer the question from pure logic in the present, not from emotion and not from your past experiences.

Can you accept the probability? Decide if you can accept the level of probability. If you can't accept the level of probability that the worst-case scenario will happen, then you will need to do something to change the situation or level of risk. For example, you want to implement an unproven strategy but if it fails, you will lose your job and put the whole company at risk. Thus, the level of probability is too high to accept. You will either need to modify the strategy or drop it all together.

Set it aside. If the level of probability is acceptable and you have also accepted the potential of the worst-case scenario, let yourself come to peace with it and set it aside.

Focus on best case. Now, with your fear out of the way, focus on your best-case scenario—what would it look, feel and sound like?

Take action. Take action toward creating your best-case scenario.

SHARPEN YOUR FOCUS

Take some time to think about what you've learned and briefly summarize that knowledge here. When you've finished reading this book, these collected thoughts will provide you with a shot of "instant" inspiration as you apply these lessons to your life.

_____

_____

_____

_____

_____

Chapter Three
Own It: No blaming,
COMPLAINING OR EXCUSES

"Take your life in your own hands, and what happens?
A terrible thing: no one to blame."
— Erica Jong

Do you feel annoyed when people complain? If so, it turns out there's a good reason why. Listening to too much complaining is bad for your brain in multiple ways, according to Trevor Blake, an entrepreneur and author of *Three Simple Steps: A Map to Success in Business and Life*. "If you're pinned in a corner for too long listening to someone being negative, you're more likely to behave that way as well."

As a Fearless Leader, you need to own it. Own it all. Own the good stuff, own the bad stuff, own how you feel and own your reactions. **Own It! No blaming, complaining or excuses is the third Fearless Leaders' success secret.**

Most people weaken themselves by blaming, complaining and making excuses. A Fearless Leader takes full responsibility, not just for successes, but for setbacks as well. When you take full responsibility, you take control of your life.

It takes strength and fortitude to admit to a mistake. There's nothing easy about it. You have to fight every natural impulse to allow yourself to be open to ridicule or judgment. It's an enormous sign of power to those around you when you can show them that you're not afraid to fail, or admit to having responsibility for what's not working in your life.

When you begin to think like a Fearless Leader, you'll see how blaming, complaining and making excuses are quite prevalent in most organizations and keep both individuals and teams underperforming. Take, for example, a conversation we had with a small business owner who had requested a training session for his sales team.

"I would love it if my sales team was coached in the Fearless Leaders' secrets," Gary, the owner, told us.

"Great," we said. "Sales professionals who apply these secrets become far better revenue producers and happier people. You do need to know though that there are some specific guidelines for participants in this program which include no blaming, complaining or making excuses during the coaching period."

Hearing this, Gary, grabbed his head with both hands above his ears as if in great agony and said, "If my sales people can't blame, complain or make excuses, I'm going to have a sales team that doesn't talk!"

Most people are just like Gary's sales team. Their default method of thinking and communicating actually disempowers them. They may complain about different aspects of their jobs, the economy, the weather, their spouse, their boss, their kids. They waste their time, energy and brainpower on what they don't control.

Whereas Fearless Leaders rarely or never indulge in this type of negativity. They understand that blaming, complaining or making excuses mentally weakens them.

The main reason for not accomplishing realistic and achievable goals that you have set is you. It's true for everyone. A lack of commitment very often becomes a breeding ground for excuses. And justifying failure to rationalize why you are not doing or achieving whatever it is you want is an all too easy habit.

Cathy's Fearless Nosedive

One of my fearless goals was to get an "A" license in skydiving. To do so, I had to complete an extensive number of jumps at various heights. I was also tested in my positioning, ability to flare (the act of slowing down the descent) and ability to land safely. Since I commit to surrounding myself with the best teachers I can find, I learned to skydive with a series of jump masters who were both active duty and former special forces team members.

The first 45 or 50 jumps I did were fairly straightforward.

One particular maneuver though always seemed to be just outside of my reach. It was a jump performed at a high altitude during which the parachute isn't actually pulled until a much lower altitude is reached (HALO - High Altitude Low Opening).

The first time I did it, I broke my toe.

The second time, I tore the meniscus in my knee.

The third and last time in May of 2006, I fractured my coccyx bone into four parts and fractured my L1 and L5 vertebrae because I passed out due to a radical change in air temperature during my decent. Unconscious, I was unable to pull the chord. When I finally came to at 800 feet off the ground, I immediately tried to push myself in the direction of the big yellow X at the landing zone. I passed out again, but fortunately had lined myself up as best as I could. Now at only 100 feet above the ground, I regained consciousness again briefly to hear everyone yelling, "Flare!"—which is a maneuver used to land. I flared too much and immediately landed on my butt so hard that I bounced off the ground.

When I was able to collect myself and take inventory of my body, I realized I was numb from the waist down. Later, I was told I had broken my sits (pelvic) bone in four places and fractured my vertebrae in two. Everyone gathered around to try to inspect my injuries, but I had no time for an examination. I needed to be in Los Angeles for a speaking engagement. I foolishly got mad at them for trying to provide medical attention. I was eventually allowed to drive home and managed to put on a suit for my event, even though my bones were literally in pieces.

That day was a valuable lesson for me. There were many opportunities to assign blame...to my instructors or to the heat. And I came pretty close to using blame to assuage my embarrassment.

But I chose to do HALO jumps knowing the dangers. Those decisions were mine. No one else's. So there was no blaming, complaining or making excuses. I chose to own all of it. As they say, no pain no gain.

Influence of Others

Even if you generally don't blame, complain or make excuses, spending too much of your time around people who do will have an undue influence on you. Do not fall into the trap of misery loves company because, in truth, alone or in company, you will be miserable.

Exercise: Steps to "Own It! No Blaming, Complaining or Making Excuses"

1. Develop awareness
- Choose something about your life that is working well. Write what it is here:

_____

- Reflect on this and own your thoughts, actions, beliefs and emotions that are helping you create this successful part of your life.

- Choose something in your life that isn't working well. Write what it is here:

_____

- What negative thoughts do you have about this situation? What actions have been taken or not taken to contribute? What are the beliefs and emotions that are helping to create the situation?

_____
_____
_____
_____

- In this situation, if you decided to own it 100 percent and take full responsibility for it, how would you think, act and feel?

_____

_____

_____

_____

- What have you learned from this exercise to increase your awareness about the value of "Own It! No Blaming, Complaining or Making Excuses"?

_____

_____

_____

_____

2. Make a decision

Decisions are the bridges between thoughts and actions. Of course, you always want to make the decision that will bring you the greatest amount of happiness and help you reach your goals. However, as much as you want that, it's not so easy to achieve. By taking responsibility for the consequences of the decisions you make, you remain more in control. Remaining in control means that you also may have the power to change the outcome.

SHARPEN YOUR FOCUS

Take some time to think about what you've learned and briefly summarize that knowledge here. When you've finished reading this book, these collected thoughts will provide you with a shot of "instant" inspiration as you apply these lessons to your life.

_____

_____

_____

_____

SECTION II: MINDSET MASTER

Chapter Four
Show Up Ready!
Aligned Minds and Extraordinary Preparation

"As a single footstep will not make a path on the Earth, so
a single thought will not make a pathway in the mind. To
make a deep physical path, we walk again and again. To
make a deep mental path, we must think over and over
the kind of thoughts we wish to dominate our lives."
-Henry David Thoreau

What gets you going with a great start? Whether you're about to close on one of the biggest sales of your career, interview for your dream job or lead an all-hands meeting to share big news, your mindset in approaching any goal-oriented situation can absolutely make or break you. Our experience in working closely with professional athletes and military special forces personnel has taught us, unequivocally, that it's essential to take control of your mindset before engaging in life's most challenging or important moments.

People who do so know what the ideal emotions are to maximize success. They create these emotions before and during an engagement, and then review in great detail how well they did. Public speaking, receiving a performance review or even arriving home after a hard day's work and getting in the right frame of mind to be with those you love are all times when your stress can be alleviated by simply learning to consciously choose and create the best thoughts, actions and emotions to optimize success in each of these situations.

Show Up Ready! is the fourth Fearless Leaders' success secret. This secret has two parts, Aligned Minds and Extraordinary Preparation.

Are You at Your Best When You Engage in the Most Important Moments of Your Life?

Fearless Leaders thrive on challenges. Their secret rests, in part, with having aligned minds. We define aligned minds as a kind of symmetry between your mental and emotional energy in both your conscious and subconscious minds.

The power of your subconscious mind is extraordinary. When you successfully align the power of both your subconscious and conscious minds you're essentially unstoppable to accomplish what you are passionate about! However, if your subconscious has a different set of goals, it will most likely triumph. This is because your subconscious mind is dominant over your conscious mind.

Here's the difference in the amount of information your two minds can process according to neuroscience research. In one second the subconscious mind can process at least 500 times the amount of information that your conscious mind can. To better understand how different the processing speeds of your two minds are, think of it as the difference between a tortoise's top speed of 2.4 mph (your conscious mind) and a fighter jet's top speed of 1,200 mph (your subconscious mind).

The greater control you have of your thoughts going into a stressful situation, the more likely you are to be at your best. This, in turn, creates the greatest possible outcome. When you have misaligned minds, your goals are conflicted which increases your stress and frustration levels. You end up underperforming because you've sabotaged yourself usually without even realizing it.

The techniques to align your minds are fairly easy to learn. Your real challenge will be to understand the subconscious beliefs and fears that may be blocking you from reaching your ultimate goals.

It may sound a little intimidating or frightening at first, but don't worry. Once you dig deep enough and discover what it is that's holding you back, your minds can ultimately be aligned for your benefit.

Fear of Success

A misalignment of your conscious and subconscious mind is often a form of fear of success. This fear is one of the most mysterious of all because many of the conflicts associated with it reside in the subconscious.

Thoughts about success in business almost always include making lots of money. Yet, both entrepreneurs and those in the corporate world often have fears or blocks to prospering. This resistance is a part of our culture and having money is often vilified. Let's analyze some of the language we use and words we hear that continually program how we think. Notice your reaction to each of these phrases as you read them:

- **Filthy rich**. Originally, this meant to be rich by dishonorable gain, but now it is used to describe someone who is very wealthy.
- **More money than God**. This is either blasphemous or means more powerful than God. Neither is a favorable perception.
- **Money is the root of all evil**…This is a common perception in our culture.

If you know you are capable of much more than what your current results are and you keep hitting walls, then you can be pretty sure you have a conscious/subconscious conflict. If you can determine what your subconscious limiting belief is, then you can resolve the conflict and free yourself.

The CEO and owner of an innovative entrepreneurial manufacturing firm who was the inventor of the patented products they manufactured once remarked, "I have worked for five years to create more structure and accountability in my business, with no success!" More structure and accountability was his conscious goal. He then did some deep subconscious work and discovered that he was sabotaging his own efforts, because he didn't want to be account-able and have to work in a lot of structure. He realized he thought that if his people had to be accountable, he did too. But he had a non-linear, right-brained inventor personality, so he unconsciously sabotaged all initiatives to increase accountability and structure in order to protect his own creative process which thrived with more freedom.

Once he realized his subconscious belief, it was easy to then solve the conscious/subconscious conflict. He said, "I'm going to be the semi-crazed eccentric inventor, work my own way and focus on inventing new products, which is what my company needs me to focus on. I'll let my management team run the company and get out of their way. They'll love this and I'll love this!"

That was the perfect solution. He invented and patented amaz-ing new products but was a horrible leader and manger by his own admission. He had a good management team, which had the poten-tial to be a great team without the chaos his personality created. He could work his strengths and his team could work their strengths. The result was the company and all involved flourished.

Joyce's Limiting Belief

We once coached a realtor named Joyce. She had been working in real estate for 10 years and was a middle-of-the-pack producer. She always had a feeling that something was holding her back, but didn't know what. After spending some time with her, we discovered that Joyce had a limiting belief formed when she was a child. She had grown up on a farm where she learned that no matter what she and her family did, if there was a drought, they couldn't squeeze a raindrop out of a cloud. If their fields were flooding, they couldn't disperse the clouds so the sun would shine.

So her child's mind created the belief, "It doesn't matter what I do, I can't affect anything." Now as a 60-something-year-old real-tor, her belief was generalized to, "It doesn't matter what marketing I do, it won't affect my sales." Through coaching, Joyce came to realize that her marketing was actually helping her sales. She did some deep work at the subconscious level of her mind and changed her belief to become, "The more I market, the more I'll sell." And that's what Joyce did. She increased her sales 279 percent in six months selling the same size houses, in the same community, in a stable market with no unusually large deals. Then three years after changing her belief, she sent us an email: "Just want you to know that 2008 and 2009, two of the worst years ever in real estate, were my two best." That's the power of aligned minds.

TC's Conflicting Goals

I sometimes struggle with a set of conflicting goals that can create a fear of success. Being my best at what I do means going on the road to deliver keynote speeches and trainings. I love doing these. But while part of me wants my work to be extraordinarily successful and to share the Fearless Leaders' success secrets globally, I also want to savor the sanctuary of my home, have private time for contemplation and be with those I love. I have to stay acutely aware of this conflict.

Over the years, we've talked with hundreds of women and men with great careers who say they constantly struggle with their desire to be successful in both their business and family lives. Misaligned minds can hold them back. If they devote themselves to their careers, are they shortchanging their families? Or if they strive to have a happy and harmonious family, will they limit their professional advancement?

Exercise: Resolving Misalignments

• Write a challenging goal that you want to achieve.

_____

_____

- List three things you do that inhibit your progress toward accomplishing your goal. For example, "I do easy, less important tasks first and they take up most of my day." Or, "I spend a lot of time worrying about things I don't control." Be specific.

- List three things you don't do that inhibit your progress toward accomplishing your goal. For example, "I don't make all the phone calls to potential customers that I could." Or, "I put off the risky things I need to do to accomplish this goal." Be specific.

- For your top "do" above, ask yourself, "What misalignments come to mind when I imagine myself doing the exact opposite?" For example, if your "do" was, "I do easy, less important tasks first and they take up most of my day," what are you in conflict about? Afraid to fail at the important tasks?

- For your top "don't do" above, ask yourself, "What misalignments come to mind when I imagine myself doing the exact opposite?" For example, if your "don't do" was, "I don't hold people accountable for their goals," your conflict about holding people accountable could be, "They won't like me if I'm tough with them" or "I don't like disagreements, they're scary."

_____

_____

_____

_____

When you identify misalignments that are hurting your success, restructure your thoughts so they address what your blocks are and also so they support you in attaining your goals.

Extraordinary Preparation is the second part of Show Up Ready! In this step you take charge of preparing yourself with a "T3" mental attitude: technically, tactically and temperamentally. This eliminates distractions and conflicts that can be obstacles to your ability to focus and to be totally present in pivotal life events.

Cathy on Prioritizing

I was honored to attend several national conventions hosted by agencies such as the National Tactical Officers Association where I participated in a number of critical programs. I learned how working warriors are taught to "prioritize life" (a term used to describe the changing status of an active shooter or hostage situation) and initiate responses required in life threatening situations. These reactions, which can be developed and measured using carefully planned training scenarios, can also help frame the qualities needed for leadership in volatile, uncertain and chaotic situations (in military/paramilitary terms they're called VUCA environments).

In the face of adversity and ambiguity, there are things we can do to make a difference in our lives, the lives of people we manage and in our communities. A Fearless Leader will undoubtedly face high-risk situations. What makes them fearless is being courageous, resilient, mindful and passionate. What makes them fearless is understanding the tangibles and intangibles of a situation, prioritizing how to face a risky situation and then excelling at implementing action.

Carol Kinsey Goman, in her book *The Nonverbal Advantage*, provides strategies on how to make a good first impression. Her initial recommendation is to become adept at consciously controlling your attitude through your thoughts and actions. People, either consciously or sub-consciously, pick up on your true emotions even when you try to hide them. Good or bad, they will then make decisions about you based on that first impression.

Researchers from New York University discovered that we make eleven major decisions about a person in the first seven seconds. They include these four:

- Is this person trustworthy?
- Are they likable?
- Are they confident?
- Are they someone worth getting to know better?

Do you use a T3 attitude to consciously control your thoughts, emotions and actions as you engage with new people? Every situation requires a slightly different mindset to optimize success. To be your best you must know what thoughts, emotions and actions help you the most and how to change them when they aren't helping you. Great preparation also increases confidence, while poor preparation can cause anxiety.

Bad starts usually lead to unhappy endings. If you don't control your actions, thoughts and emotions then you may be hurting yourself by decreasing or eliminating your T3 attitude opportunities to be successful in those crucial, potentially life-changing moments.

Which leader engenders confidence in others? The one who is anxious or the one who is confident? Who usually sells more, the sales rep who is fearful or the one who is relaxed?

Take a moment to think about the following scenarios. How profound of an effect do you think the right focus would have in each situation as opposed to a setting that doesn't allow you to fully engage? What would be the most important thoughts or emotions when:

- Leading a team meeting?
- Talking with your boss?
- Arriving at work in the morning?
- Arriving at home in the evening or after a trip?
- Resolving a conflict with someone you love?
- Engaging in a new project?
- Giving a speech?

Gain Control with a T3 Mental Attitude

The more you gain control of your thoughts, and thus your emotions and mindset, when going into a stressful situation, the more likely you are to create the best outcome. Let's go into depth on the three categories of a T3 attitude: technical, tactical and temperamental.

Technical Preparation

One of the most popular articles we have written was *The Warren Buffett/Peyton Manning Secret Success Strategy*. Warren Buffett, possibly the best stock market investor of all time, and Manning, one of the greatest National Football League quarterbacks of all time, are both masters of preparation and seizing opportunities.

They research, study and find ways to capitalize on opportunities that others don't. In Warren Buffett's 1984 speech, "The Superinvestors of Graham-and-Doddsville" at Columbia University, he stated his success strategy for choosing companies to invest in was to "...search for discrepancies between the value of a business and the price of small pieces of that business in the market...exploit those discrepancies without the efficient market theorist's concern as to whether it is January, or July..."

Similarly, Peyton Manning breaks down NFL defenses not just by looking for the basic opportunity to exploit them in general, but also by finding opportunities at the individual defensive player level.

Jim Mora, who coached Manning for four years, said this about him: "What sets Manning apart is his preparation. That's it in a word: preparation. He prepares himself mentally, physically and emotionally to be the best he can be. Now everyone wants to be the best. But Peyton does what it takes to be the best. There's a difference."

How might you use this strategy? It will be a little different for each person, just like it's different for Buffett and Manning. Here's how one local, and soon to be superstar, entrepreneur has used it. Let's call him John.

John identified a niche Microsoft software product that was growing market share quickly. He also discovered that for every $10,000 spent on the software, there was a $100,000 consulting/ training opportunity to install and train employees on the use of the software. John's firm was a perfect fit to be the high-tech consulting/training partner. After a couple of years, John's firm is now on the way to becoming the largest consulting/training business in this segment.

Tactical Preparation

In sports and in the military, physical preparation is obvious because you need a highly trained body. But how about to be highly effective as a leader, as a manager, in sales, as an entrepreneur, as a humanitarian or even being a parent leading your children? The physical aspects of being great in these situations are much less obvious but still vital.

In all of these cases, optimizing the use of your mind by optimizing your body and energy involves several elements: the quantity and quality of your sleep; your fitness level; your nutrition; the amount of water you drink; and you preparing your body to support your mind to be it's best when you most need it. When you take good care of your body, you have more energy and greater mental clarity to give you an important edge.

Temperamental Preparation

Creating the right thoughts, emotions and mindset in the most challenging personal or professional situations gives you an advantage for success and happiness that others can only wish for. Mental and emotional preparations are critically important for achieving your dreams.

Mental and emotional preparation techniques are all fairly easy to learn and can be mastered if you apply them consciously for a long enough period of time. Remember, when mentally preparing, you are either wiring or rewiring your brain so you can be your best. Precision and repetition are crucial. You can use the techniques you have already learned to get yourself prepared. But first, choose what thoughts and emotions you want to have that you believe will help you the most. Let's say you want to be confident and relaxed. Then, like you learned in the first chapter, if you access a confident relaxed memory, you can create that emotion.

Additionally, like champion skier Jeremy Bloom who has an amazing level of mind mastery, you can choose the one key that is most important to focus on for a great start. He focused on making a good turn in the first six inches of the course.

Use Pre-event Routines to Prepare

When talking with one of the top junior figure skaters in the U.S., she said, "Sometimes in competitions I skate great and nail all my jumps effortlessly. But sometimes I don't and I don't know why." In a coaching conversation, she realized that she competed best when she was the first one to skate after the warm-up session. In figure skating competitions though, skaters warm up in small groups and then each is randomly assigned to when they will skate first, second, third, or so on after the warm-up. She skated her worst in competitions when she skated last after the warm-up because she had physically cooled off and tightened up.

She identified that a combination of stretching exercises, running in place on her skates and moving her body as she imagined going through her routine helped to keep her ready to compete. This solved her competitive inconsistencies and it no longer mattered when she skated after her warm-up. She had a pre-event routine that allowed her to always show up ready!

Phil Mickelson, a top ranked professional golfer for many years, performs a highly practiced, multi-step routine before he takes a shot in a competition. Before a race, Olympic athlete Lindsey Vonn, considered to be the best woman skier in U.S. history, creates a mental image of skiing the most perfect run she can. Kobe Bryant, MVP of the 2009-2010 NBA finals, always does exactly the same routine before each free throw. Why do world-class athletes practice to perfect their pre-event routines? Because they perform better when they do.

What's your pre-routine? If you lead, sell or manage, do you have a routine to be your best? How about when you speak to groups, make a critical phone call, give feedback to help someone who has made a major mistake? Are you more likely to be ready to "knock 'em dead" or wish you were dead due to fear and embarrassment you might blow it?

If great athletes in all sports use routines to get their minds and bodies maximally prepared for success, why don't the rest of us use routines to help us be more courageous, confident or relaxed?

Goal of a T3 Pre-routine

You can use a pre-routine to get you in the right mindset and at the energy level to be your best in any specific situation. Preparing using a pre-routine will create much greater success and joy in all of the most important situations you have in your life.

Example of a T3 Pre-routine in Leadership

Imagine a pre-presentation to a whole company, organization, division or your team, whatever size it is. It will also apply to any important conversation you're going to engage in even at the individual level.

Technical. Do your research. Have all the background information you need to be accurate to backup what you'll say. Anticipate questions and develop well thought-out answers for each. This is especially important for the questions you hope no one asks. Be especially prepared to answer these. Practice answering the questions you might receive until you feel very confident in your answers.

Tactical. Sleep well, especially two nights before. Be hydrated. The brain and body function best when well hydrated. Use your breathing pattern to either bring more energy into your body by using sharp deep, quick inhalations and exhalations, or relax your body by using slow, deep inhalations and even slower exhalations. In the hours leading up to presentation, avoid carbohydrates and eat some protein to keep your blood sugar level even and provide continued energy for your brain.

Temperamental. Identify the thoughts, emotions and keys that will create the greatest success. If you are sharing good news, or anything you want to create excitement around, you need to have authentic excitement in yourself before you engage. That might be an emotional key. Your thought could be something like, "I will share my enthusiasm for this and answer every question they have, until everyone begins to share my enthusiasm with me." Using thoughts, emotions and keys, imagine as precisely as possible having an amazingly successful presentation.

In the article recounted below entitled *Person of the Year 2011* for *Time* magazine, Admiral William McRaven was rightfully honored. As you read this overview, ponder how much, technical, tactical and temperamental preparation had to take place for the described mission to be successful:

Admiral McRaven and his SEAL team had been training for the possibility of a mission where they would have to parachute unnoticed from high altitude (over 10,000 feet). Earlier, during a practice jump, he collided with the chute of one of his team members during a 100 mph free fall, got tangled in his chute's chords as it opened and in his words, "it split me like a nutcracker." So it was not under the command of McRaven, who was recovering from his injuries, when Naval Special Warfare Group 1 began the search for Osama bin Laden after the al-Qaeda attacks on September 11, 2001.

A decade after the al-Qaeda attacks, McRaven had already recovered and resumed his ranks. He and his team showed up ready. By then, a three-star admiral atop the Joint Special Operations Command (JSOC), McRaven and his team took on the mission to "finish options" for the elusive bin Laden. It was May 1, 2011 when McRaven commanded the helicopter assault against the al-Qaeda leader in Abbottobad, Pakistan.

Others remember McRaven as calm as can be as he reported happenings in real time to President Obama. Even when the lead helicopter crash-landed, McRaven simply said with no expression, "As you see, we have a helicopter down."

Barton Gellman, the author of this *Time* magazine piece, describes: "Toward the end, with the assault team moving from room to room, McRaven stepped unexpectedly away from the screen. An unnerving silence descended as the camera stayed on the admiral's empty chair, his habitual yellow can of Rip It energy drink in the foreground. Then McRaven swung back into the picture. 'I want to confirm we have a call of Geronimo EKIA,' he said evenly." And then it was over. bin Laden was now the "enemy killed in action" and in the hands of America. Extraordinary T3 preparation and staying present in the moment paid off. Mission accomplished.

Show Up Ready! Checklist

Choose the next situation where you want to make sure you're at your best and prepare using this 10 point checklist.

1. _____ I'm fully committed to the success of this goal!

2. _____ I've paid close attention to my thoughts and body's reaction and my minds are aligned, or I'm very aware of conflicting goals and I'm making sure that both sets of goals are being met.

3. ____ I'm aware of any fears I have and have dealt with them so that they are not in control of me, but rather I'm in control of them.

4. ____ I know what I need to do for a successful start and am confident in implementing my plan.

5. ____ I have a pre-routine that I will use that allows me to be at my best.

6. ____ I am confident in my preparation.

7. ____ I have a plan on how to physically be prepared including sleep, hydration, nutrition and exercise.

8. ____ I know the thoughts I need to focus on before and as I begin.

9. ____I have repeatedly mentally rehearsed being successful.

10. ____ I feel completely ready.

SHARPEN YOUR FOCUS

Take some time to think about what you've learned and briefly summarize that knowledge here. When you've finished reading this book, these collected thoughts will provide you with a shot of "instant" inspiration as you apply these lessons to your life.

_____

_____

_____

_____

_____

CHAPTER FIVE
BE A MASTER OF MIND
CONTROL

"A man is but the product of his thoughts."
– Mahatma Gandhi

Early research indicated that emotional resilience was limited to a very small group of individuals. But more recently it has become evident that this resiliency is much more prevalent. What characteristics give individuals the ability to withstand adverse circumstances that can destroy the resolve of others?

In 2009, the U.S. Department of the Army established the Comprehensive Soldier Fitness (CSF) program with the goal of enhancing "the resilience, readiness and potential of soldiers." According to a report from Peter W. Chiarelli, U.S. Army Vice Chief of Staff, the CSF program emphasizes "human potential through a focus on positive emotions, traits, institutions, and social relationships." In short, a soldier learns to banish negativity by centering on what is good in their life.

We are all imperfect beings. Even the most high-achieving business leaders, military professionals and Olympic athletes have negative or fearful thoughts that can sabotage their success. The difference between them and others is that they continually use two very important steps to overcome their insecurities and doubts. The first is to recognize when they have destructive thoughts, and the second is to have a process in which they reframe that negativity.

What are the Benefits of Becoming a Master of Mind Control?

If you master control of your actions, thoughts and emotions in each moment:

- You will have more command over all you actually have direct control of.
- You will continually be at your best.
- You will have enormous personal power.
- You will create a consciousness that allows you to excel as a leader.
- You will continue to improve your mental conditioning to achieve what's important to you.
- You will learn to not sabotage yourself.
- You will ultimately create greater success and happiness for yourself.

Without mastery of your mind, you can easily fall victim to your own undisciplined thoughts. Out of control in the most important moments of your life, you will most likely be unfocused and/or living in the past or future. The effect of surrendering to your negative thoughts will result in a minimized or completely sabotaged success. By limiting your progress, you also decrease your joy and happiness.

Anyone can learn the techniques in this chapter because they are as simple as they are profoundly effective. Yet mastery will take time and commitment on your part, but they will give you the ability to continually improve your mental conditioning. You will think and feel more of how you would like to and be more in the present moment.

Being the master of your mind can do more than increase your career success; as Navy SEAL Marcus Luttrell discovered, it can save your life. Following a battle in the mountains on the border between Pakistan and Afghanistan that left him badly injured and the sole survivor from his team, Luttrell made his painful way seven miles to where he was discovered by the Pashtun civilians who would protect him and care for his terrible injuries. He had initially expected them to turn him over to the Taliban. Instead though, bound by the tradition of *lokhay*, they made what he called "an unbreakable commitment to defend [him] to the death. And not just the death of the principal tribesman or family who made the original commitment...the whole damned village." But, even as he waited to be either killed by the Taliban or rescued by his fellow Marines, he refused to dwell on the past or his future, maintaining mastery of his mind and remaining in the moment.

Do you consciously choose to focus on what's positive in your life? Are you at your personal best under stress? Are you the master or the victim of your own mind? If you had control of your thoughts, actions and emotions in each moment, how would you be different? How would your entire life be different? How much better do you think it could be?

Learn to control your own mind in the present, even under tremendous pressure. **Be a master of mind control is the fifth Fearless Leaders' success secret.**

To be a Fearless Leader means you are able to stay in control and focused in the present because you have a unique belief in your own conscious and subconscious minds when most other people don't. You are master of your mind and don't allow yourself to become ruled by unrealistic fears or unfounded negative thoughts.

The last chapter focused on preparation to be your best when it counts the most in your life. This chapter focuses on how to stay present, with the right thoughts and emotions to be your best when it most counts, as well as how to be more resilient.

A Four-step Thought Replacement Technique

Here are four brief steps to replace destructive, negative or fearful thoughts with constructive ones to better control your mind:

Recognize the destructive thoughts.
Pause and Reset the destructive thoughts.

Replace the destructive thoughts with constructive thoughts.

Reward/Enjoy yourself for gaining control of your mind!

You have to first recognize when you have destructive thoughts. You have so many thoughts during the day, most of them originating in your subconscious mind, that it's nearly impossible to notice them all. But it's imperative for you to be able to pinpoint them when they occur. Examples might sound something like:

I really stink at...

I can't...

That scares me!

These destructive thoughts are all based on fear or worry, rather than possibility. They block you from achieving what you're capable of.

Three Ways to Recognize Your Destructive Thoughts

Your capacity to observe your thoughts is actually one of the amazing abilities of your most evolved part of your brain, often referred to as the executive brain, which is located in the frontal lobe. Strengthening the observer-self is an extremely important aspect of mastering your mind. Here are three ways to identify negative, destructive or fearful thoughts:

Hear them. You can hear these thoughts going through your mind when you're paying attention to what you are thinking.

Feel them. You can't feel these thoughts directly, but you can notice them by feeling the physical reaction they create—tension in your shoulders, sweaty hands, shallow breathing in your chest, tightness in your stomach.

See them. Well, you can't see them either. But what you can see is you procrastinating. What is your inaction telling you? Most likely, it's saying that you're scared.

Mind Like a River

There's also an advanced technique for controlling your thoughts that champion skier Jeremy Bloom uses. He calls it the "Mind Like a River" approach.

He said, "I think it's pretty normal for athletes to have self-defeating thoughts [like] you will be visualizing your run and you'll fall. And what I learned, when I think I really started to dominate the sport and really ski to my potential, was when I employed this mentality of—I called it 'Mind Like a River.' And I just visualized this free-flowing river through my head and through my brain. And I really wouldn't allow anything to attach, so feelings of self-defeat or concerns flowed through my head. When I really achieved the best mental position that I ever had was when my mind was like a river and I built a tunnel around what was important and the things outside of that tunnel never got in. If they would, they'd just flow right out. Very simple."

Exercise: Mind Like a River Practice

- Sit comfortably and allow yourself to relax. To help you relax, take some slow, deep breaths with your exhalations being longer than your inhalations.

- Imagine a free-flowing river running through your mind that nothing can attach to. Any thought that comes into your mind is just gently carried away by the current, except for the ones you chose to focus on. For Bloom, in the starting gate it was the first six inches of the course.

- If you lose your focus or get distracted, let the distraction float away on the river and refocus.

- After a period of time of your choosing, see what you notice about your body and mind.

This thought replacement technique keeps you focused on what you do want instead of on what you fear or don't want. When you have a well developed observer-self and have better control of your thoughts, you'll also notice that you stop having such strong emotional reactions to what others say, or to the adversities and losses you experience.

Cathy's Inspiration

There is a very special verse by an anonymous author that I read to my daughter. "As you grow up, you will have your heart broken more than once and it's harder every time. You'll break hearts too, so remember how it felt when yours was broken. You'll fight with your best friend. You'll cry because time is passing too fast and you'll eventually lose someone you love. So take too many pictures, laugh too much and love like you've never been hurt, because every 60 seconds you spend upset is a minute of happiness you'll never get back."

Your Observer-self Noting Your Physiological Responses

To master your mind, you will want to use your observer-self to pay attention to your physiological responses as well as to your thoughts. For example, it's important to learn to monitor your breath. How are you breathing? Shallow and rapid in your upper chest? Or, slow and deep all the way down into your abdomen? Your breathing is a direct reflection of how tense or relaxed you are. Monitoring your breathing also gives you the ability to directly control your own excitation or relaxation levels. By taking slow, deep breaths into your abdomen, you decrease the level of excitement or tension in your body. When you replace your negative, destructive or fearful thoughts with positive ones and you deepen and slow your breathing, you benefit exponentially by combining the mind and body working together.

How an NFL Linebacker Used Thought Replacement

Former Denver Bronco football player Karl Mecklenburg is one of our Fearless Leaders. He played 13 years for the Denver Broncos, was a six-time Pro Bowl selection and captain of the team for several years despite being told during most of his career that they were bringing in bigger, faster, stronger players than him and, "You probably wouldn't make the team." Mecklenburg kept his focus on one thing though, "To be the best football player ever." It was his continuous mantra and he never swayed from it.

Mecklenburg understood setbacks and how to reframe/rethink them. He said, "Success is overcoming obstacles. If you are not running into problems, you're not pushing hard enough. You should expect and anticipate problems—maybe not enjoy them, but learn from them. You can always learn more from what you did wrong, than what you did right—because sometimes when things go right, it's just that the stars lined up."

Anytime Mecklenburg had a negative or fearful thought, he replaced it with his one focusing thought, "To be the best football player ever."

The Navy SEAL Ethos

Working with Navy Special Warfare (NSW) has been one of the most rewarding aspects of our work. NSW is comprised of two major groups of special operators: the SEAL's (Sea, Air, Land) and SWCC (Special Warfare Combatant Craft Crewman). While both of these fearless teams share the same warrior ethos working together on missions with SWCC inserting and extracting their SEAL colleagues, they are only distinguishable by their team credo. Below is the most well known Navy SEAL credo that represents the common attitudes, beliefs and characteristics of these extraordinary individuals serving our nation:

In times of war or uncertainty there is a special breed of warrior ready to answer our Nation's call. A common man with uncommon desire to succeed. Forged by adversity, he stands alongside America's finest special operations forces to serve his country, the American people, and protect their way of life. I am that man.

My Trident is a symbol of honor and heritage. Bestowed upon me by the heroes that have gone before, it embodies the trust of those I have sworn to protect. By wearing the Trident I accept the responsibility of my chosen profession and way of life. It is a privilege that I must earn every day. My loyalty to Country and Team is beyond reproach. I humbly serve as a guardian to my fellow Americans always ready to defend those who are unable to defend themselves. I do not advertise the nature of my work, nor seek recognition for my actions. I voluntarily accept the inherent hazards of my profession, placing the welfare and security of others before my own. I serve with honor on and off the battlefield. The ability to control my emotions and my actions, regardless of circumstance, sets me apart from other men. Uncompromising integrity is my standard. My character and honor are steadfast. My word is my bond.

We expect to lead and be led. In the absence of orders I will take charge, lead my teammates and accomplish the mission. I lead by example in all situations. I will never quit. I persevere and thrive on adversity. My Nation expects me to be physically harder and mentally stronger than my enemies. If knocked down, I will get back up, every time. I will draw on every remaining ounce of strength to protect my teammates and to accomplish our mission. I am never out of the fight.

We demand discipline. We expect innovation. The lives of my teammates and the success of our mission depend on me—my technical skill, tactical proficiency, and attention to detail. My training is never complete. We train for war and fight to win. I stand ready to bring the full spectrum of combat power to bear in order to achieve my mission and the goals established by my country. The execution of my duties will be swift and violent when required yet guided by the very principles that I serve to defend. Brave men have fought and died building the proud tradition and feared reputation that I am bound to uphold. In the worst of conditions, the legacy of my teammates steadies my resolve and silently guides my every deed. I will not fail.

Being in the SEAL/SWCC program is not about physical size, it's about heart and mental conditioning. In fact, their mental training is even more important than their physical training.

The SWCC motto sharpens the focus of these working warriors in one simple statement: "On Time, On Target, Never Quit." The military spends millions of dollars to create Navy SEAL/SWCC forces, among other special operations units like, Second Recon Marines, Army Rangers, Delta Force and Army Special Operations Aviation Regiment (SOAR).

Though being quiet professionals is a part of their credo, recent events have put these patriots at the center of attention in the media, including blockbuster books and movies. These working warriors take pride in not looking for recognition. This is part of their mental training. They are taught to focus on their goal, never their own glory. In fact, doing anything bringing attention to the self in the context of being a special operations team member will get that person pushed out of that community fast.

Cathy Pays Tribute

While I am not a military professional, I am a behavioral scientist who has been fortunate to be asked to share my insights on the subject of leadership development and emotional and social intelligence with this community in support of future leaders across the Joint Special Operations Forces (JSOF). Through the trust and relationships that have been built, in some small way, I take comfort in knowing I have contributed to their evolving role in a growing environment of joint operational effectiveness More importantly, I do this work largely in service to the memory of my father, Lieutenant Commander Bernard Greenberg, who served in Korea and was reported to have contributed to the success of several underwater demolition missions.

Here are more techniques to help you master your mind:

Technique 1 - Mental Rehearsal

Mental rehearsal is a very powerful self-transformational tool that science has proven to be highly effective at accelerating learning and strengthening focus to bring into reality what you want. Sports psychology has been at the leading edge of the use of mental rehearsal. There are over a hundred studies demonstrating that when mental rehearsal is used correctly it can improve performance.

The scientific documentation on brain blood flow suggests that the prefrontal lobes of the brain (the executive brain) reacts the same to just thinking about doing something as it does to actually doing something. Thus, images and thoughts you give to your brain become your subconscious guide. The more often your images are reinforced, the stronger they are imprinted in your conscious and subconscious minds, and the more likely you will be to live out this image in reality.

Surgeons, special operations military personnel and humanitarians among others all use mental rehearsal to help them be more successful. Mental rehearsal includes the use of all of our senses: seeing, feeling, hearing, tasting and smelling. When you can combine these senses and fully imagine the mental image of your goal, it can be yours to attain.

To prepare yourself for mental rehearsal, you may want to start with a centering breath. A centering breath can be taken at any time when you feel that you would like to focus your energy more constructively on what you are doing. It's relaxing. Good opportunities to use the centering breath include: the time leading up to an important performance, before making a phone call, before answering the phone, before an important meeting, before answering a question that is important to you, before responding during a conflict with someone...before doing anything that is important to you. It only takes from six to fifteen seconds and since you need to breathe anyway, you might as well take control of your mind and body at the same time.

Technique 2 - The Centering Breath Process

Take a moderately deep breath into your abdominal area for approximately four seconds.

Release your breath slowly over four to ten seconds, and let your shoulders, face and neck relax as your energy focuses in your lower abdominal area. Let the tension drain away.

Think of a very pleasant thought or focus on what you need to. **Do this as often as you would like.**

Exercise: Three Levels of Mental Rehearsal

For each level choose to imagine doing something that's important to you as best as you can. It could be leading a meeting, having a sales conversation, confronting a colleague, asking for something you really want or feeling more confident. For this exercise, we'll call it "the event."

Level 1
- Choose what you want to mentally practice (the event).
- Take a centering breath.
- Imagine doing the event to the best of your ability.

Level 2
- Choose what you want to mentally practice and the emotions that will maximize your success.
- Take a centering breath.
- In order to create the right emotions and to program the correct part of your brain, create the feelings that are most important in order for you to be successful in this event. For example, if you want to feel confidence in the event, remember a time when you were confident so that you are now in the "confident" neural network of your mind.
- Once you can feel some of the emotion you want to create, imagine being your best in the event.

Level 3

This is the most sophisticated level of mental rehearsal and reflects recent science on how to maximize its effectiveness.

Body. Do your mental rehearsal replicating as closely as possible your body position, posture and movement that you will use in the event. Will you be seated, standing, moving, interacting?

Environment. Imagine a physical environment as close to the actual environment you will be in. Is it noisy, quiet, hot, cold, inside or outside? Replicate it as much as possible, the more realistic, the better.

Focus. Imagine focusing your attention on the same things you would when engaged in the situation you are rehearsing. If you are selling, or in any conversation with another person or very small group, imagine focusing on the person or persons you are talking with. Imagine looking them in the eye, just as you would when in-person. Imagine moving your focus and their focus to something that you want them to see.

Timing. Imagine the whole event in real time or choose part of the event and imagine it in real time. For example, if you are running a meeting, you might imagine in real time the beginning and each critical point.

Emotion. To re-emphasize, your mental rehearsal should involve the emotions that you would feel when engaged in the real situation. Do you want to be relaxed, energized, excited? This may be the most important piece of your mental rehearsal. If you have and project the emotions that allow you to be your best you can get away with other mistakes. For example, many sales organizations focus on and prepare indivudals only for the "close" and as a result of focusing on the "close" they create "anxiety" rather than "confidence." Whereas in paramilitary or military scenarios, working warriors are run through situations over and over to create a sense of "confidence" under different conditions and as a result create "energy" and often "excitement" at the thought of an opportunity to display their talents. If you show up in the wrong emotional state, you won't be at your best, period. Nothing will change that.

All countries that have Olympic training centers teach their athletes how to stay present, positive and focused under the stress of competition and how to be resilient when they lose. We teach military and paramilitary professionals who lay their lives on the line, and athletes who sometimes compete in front of millions of people, how to stay present and positive under stress. If they can learn to be present and resilient under the extreme stress they face, we believe you can as well under your most challenging situations.

SHARPEN YOUR FOCUS

Take some time to think about how you can be more in control of your mind in the present moment? How can you apply the techniques in this chapter? Then briefly summarize that knowledge here. When you've finished reading this book, these collected thoughts will provide you with a shot of "instant" inspiration as you apply these lessons to your life.

_____

_____

_____

_____

_____

CHAPTER SIX
VALUE CRITICAL REVIEW

"Feedback is the breakfast of champions."
-Ken Blanchard, author and management expert

What's your greatest learning opportunity? If you ask a professional athlete or military leader most would tell you in their own way, "It's my critical review of each of my experiences, especially those that went badly." Professional athletes and great performers watch videos of themselves or their team and then make critical evaluations so they can improve. In developing your leadership, management and interpersonal skills, how often do you watch video of yourself? How often do you receive objective feedback from a person or group of people you respect and trust?

If you were a world-class athlete, you would review video with your coach of all of your competitions and even of some of your practices. As a leader in any field, you'd benefit the same way an elite athlete benefits by having a coach give you detailed feedback on all of your most important challenges.

An after-action review technique can help you identify more of the small things, the nuances, that will help you become better. It's improving all the little things that allows you to go from being good to being great.

In business, most of the feedback you receive is fairly general. It's the equivalent of a professional athlete's coach only reviewing the performance at the end of a season. For example, compare the coaching of a world-class athlete to what a business leader typically receives after making a mistake such as having a deal go bad.

Anybody with a well adjusted mindset though will optimize every learning opportunity and knows that mistakes and losses are great learning opportunities. These people intimately understand the importance of being resilient, breaking everything down under a microscope and analyzing every move. **They value critical review, which is the sixth Fearless Leaders' success secret.**

This Mindset Master section has three time frames: before, during and after an important event. So far you have learned what to do before engaging in your important events—how to Show Up Ready! You've learned how to stay in the present moment under stress using mind control. And this chapter completes the Mindset Master section by providing you with a technique to accelerate your development through learning from both your successes and particularly from your mistakes and setbacks.

The Business After-action Review

In a typical business review process after something has gone badly, if it's even done, the conversation is generally negative, depressing and demotivating. In these business after-action reviews, almost all the time is spent on what went wrong rather than on what went right and how to improve. Very little time, if any, is spent on mentally, emotionally, physically or technically correcting mistakes. In military terms it's called a "hot wash." While it's meant to highlight key strengths and weaknesses, it leads more toward negativity.

Whereas when we asked Karl Mecklenburg about his critical evaluation process, he said, "Everybody else would watch the film. But I watched it in greater detail. And when everyone else was done, I would pick the three things that I made the biggest mistakes with and then I would commit to those three things to improve on during the week. And the way I would improve is I would physically practice—but mostly what I would do is I would mentally rehearse constantly...I would practice it hundreds and hundreds of times, over and over in my mind."

Mecklenburg's mental process in dealing with mistakes is the opposite of beating yourself up. He was brutally honest with himself about his mistakes, but poured his physical, mental and emotional energy into correcting his errors. He used massive amounts of mental repetition to retrain his mind and body creating a new mental and physical pattern to instinctively make the right moves on the field.

He credits this mental training as being a big part of his success. Like Mecklenburg, you too can do this for the skills that are important to your success. When you identify something you want to improve, mentally practice it over and over until you have created a new, strong neural pathway in your brain.

Fearless Leaders appreciate critical review as long as it is constructive and actionable. This secret optimizes rapid in-depth learning because you can improve from both the situations in your life that work out well and from those that don't. You can also appreciate that success is transformed failure.

Most people want to forget about things that don't go well. Or worse, they ruminate on the mistake which only strengthens the neural pathway that remembers how to make the mistake, thus making it more likely they will repeat it. Fearless Leaders don't do this. They are resilient and want to improve or change the strategies that failed, their bad performances and the times they messed up.

Champion skier Jeremy Bloom said, "I love setbacks!" Because Bloom knew that when he, or his team had a tough setback it was an enormous learning opportunity that he would take advantage of and others wouldn't to the degree he did, thus giving him/his team an advantage.

This technique can help you too create your own competitive advantage because the speed at which you and your team learns, changes and adapts is a large factor in your success. If you are in sales, this is a way to evaluate your performance just as an athlete does when watching video. You likely will not have video of yourself, so you will have to use your mind and members of your team to provide you with an objective reflection of what you did and how you did it.

No matter what the scenario, you can apply this like all of the Fearless Leaders' success secrets to get better at anything that is important to you.

Below is a powerful technique you can use yourself or with your team to optimize learning, especially with mistakes and setbacks:

Technique - Rewind/Review/Take2

Rewind. In your mind, rewind back to *before* the mistake, or setback occurred— often there was an accumulation of small things that took place before the actual mistake happened. Always go back and examine your beliefs and assumptions. Often this is where it all began.

Review. In the greatest detail you can, replay every aspect of what took place— every little nuance that added up to the end result. This is the equivalent of the professional sports team watching video of their games in almost microscopic detail.

Take2. Begin by defining the ideal scenario instead of the mistake. Then see, feel, hear and imagine every nuance of what your ideal scenario would be like (this is your first retake). Keep imagining the ideal in your mind to create new neural pathways and new thinking patterns. Then, the next time you are in a similar situation, the strongest neural pathway in your mind will be the ideal scenario, not the mistake.

Rewind/Review/Take2 is a time-tested learning technique that is incredibly effective when applied in business and personal development. If you are a person who continually works to improve, it can become a very powerful tool for you.

How might you, your team or organization utilize the Rewind/Review/Take2 technique after all of your challenges?

Exercise: Rewind/Review/Take2 Practice

- What was the last big mistake you made?

  _____

- Rewind back to how you thought, felt, acted and believed that
  helped to set up that mistake.

  _____

  _____

  _____

  _____

- Review in detail the whole timeline from the earliest part of
  your rewind through your mistake. Write down all you notice
  that compounded the mistake including how you contributed
  and what external factors such as other people or environment
  played a part.

  _____

  _____

  _____

  _____

- Identify what would be the ideal scenario to correct the mistake
  made.

  _____

  _____

  _____

  _____

- Imagine (see, feel and hear) every nuance of what your ideal
  scenario would be like if you got a do-over. Repeat over and over
  to build a new neural pathway in your brain.

- Acknowledge yourself for continuing to develop mastery of
  your mind.

- As you gain more control of your mind, you can also learn to be more mindful and think with a higher level of consciousness. This is what you will learn to do in the next section entitled "Mindfulness."

SHARPEN YOUR FOCUS

Take some time to think about what you've learned and briefly summarize that knowledge here. When you've finished reading this book, these collected thoughts will provide you with a shot of "instant" inspiration as you apply these lessons to your life.

_____

_____

_____

_____

_____

SECTION III: MINDFULNESS

CHAPTER SEVEN
THINK WITH MINDFULNESS

"Mindfulness is simply being aware of what is happening right now
without wishing it were different; enjoying the pleasant without
holding on when it changes (which it will); being with the unpleas-
ant without fearing it will always be this way (which it won't)."

– James Baraz

If you could take a pill that would decrease your negative thoughts,
mind chatter, worry and lack of focus, would you take it? Many
people would. These positive changes in states of mind can be
attained, but not from a pill. Rather, they are the benefits from
engaging in a mindful practice. John Kabat-Zinn, a leader in the
use of mindfulness meditation in medicine, sees parallels between
the mind and the great oceans. Waves of emotion may roil the surface, but 30 feet below it is calm. By turning inward and tuning into
your every breath as it moves through your body, you can take a
deeper, more serene dive into your own inner "oasis."

According to *Scientific American Mind* (April 2013), mindfulness, or being keenly aware of the present without judgment, can
positively impact your mood, hone your focus and improve your
health. The research shows that the development of mindfulness
decreases the release of cortisol, often referred to as the stress
hormone. Lower levels of cortisol are associated with feelings of
relaxation, contentment and inner peace. Mindfulness also allows
us to essentially be happier and healthier people. *Time* magazine
brought further support to this practice in a February 3, 2014 cover
story entitled "The Mindful Revolution."

Some of the psychophysiological benefits of mindfulness training that research supports include:

Decreased stress (feeling less pressure to perform)
Decreased anxiety (better emotional control)
Decreased worry (feeling more positive)
Decreased emotional reactivity (better impulse control)
Decreased depression (feeling more hopeful)
Decreased blood pressure (feeling more calm)
Decreased chronic pain (feeling less discomfort)
Increased focus (feeling more mentally aware)
Increased ability to handle distractions (feeling more centered)
Increased empathy (feeling more compassionate)
Improved immune system functions (better health)
Improved digestive functions (better nutrition)
Improved working memory (better brain power)
Improved concentration (better problem solving and decision-making)
Improved quality of sleep (better overall wellbeing)

It's pretty amazing how extensive the benefits of mindfulness training are for your mind, body and spirit. It wasn't many years ago when an executive said to us, "Why would I ever want to run if I wasn't playing a sport or a game?" Now, most executives recognize the many mind/body benefits from physical activity. We believe the importance of training your mind will follow a similar course to the importance of training your body.

Alexander Weiss, a comparative psychologist in Edinburgh, Scotland has noted that researchers have recognized for many years that people who are agreeable and happy, and low on neuroticism (characterized by anxiety, moodiness, worry, envy and jealousy) generally enjoy more successful lives, live longer and have healthier immune systems. While the opposite is true of people who behave otherwise as studies show they have less overall successful lives and are more inclined to have poor immune functions. This is due to the negative biological byproducts of these character traits according to a February 2014 *Psychology Today* article by Virginia Morell.

Even Harvard Business School teaches mindfulness. Many of our highly respected leaders have already been developing mindfulness for years; because being mindful is powerful. Imagine talking with a person who is so present and engaged with you nothing else seems to exist. One who listens to your opinions with appreciation and without judgment. This is what it's like talking with someone being mindful in a conversation with you. It's powerful in all interpersonal interactions. **Think with mindfulness is the seventh Fearless Leaders' success secret.**

In the Present Moment

The undisciplined mind wanders to the past, the future, to different thoughts. Stay in the moment with your experience. The present is the most powerful time you have and savoring the important nuances of the moment expands your mind.

In mindfulness, though you focus on the now, it doesn't mean you can't think about the past or future. You can think about the past or future mindfully and purposefully with full awareness of your thoughts, emotions and actions. You simply do so by learning to eliminate the distractions they can cause.

Cathy on Paying Attention

Losing, even temporarily, your ability to be mindful can have potentially devastating results. In 1996, I was six months pregnant and, although feeling distinctly unwell, decided to facilitate what was a very important meeting for a global director of JP Morgan. Two days prior to the meeting, a nurse practitioner had told me that the heartbeat of the fetus I was carrying was undetectable. She told me, "Don't panic, this happens. I'll discuss it with the doctor." I had told myself that either the baby would be all right or it wouldn't—I had to fulfill my commitments. I became more and more ill, but I had such a fear I wouldn't be trusted and valued by my colleagues or my clients if I didn't show up, that I forced myself to make the nearly three hour drive and meet with the team as planned.

During the break for lunch, a message from the doctor's office informed me that the baby had passed sometime prior to my last obstetrician appointment and that I was in a condition known as toxic shock. With the terrible and frightening news, did I immediately leave the meeting and go to the hospital for critical medical care? No, this was one of the most important engagements of my career. I remained focused on my commitment, set an example for my team, finished the meeting and then went to the hospital. And even as I was admitted and underwent a week of medical care including transfusions to cleanse my body of toxins, all that I could think about was the deliverables I had promised to my client.

Later, during a period of self-reflection, I realized that I should have been paying close attention to what was most important in the moment, my health and wellbeing, rather than worrying about the team, my future and what it held for my client. In fact, when my client heard about my situation afterwards, they were more than concerned and went above and beyond to comfort my fears.

The practice of mindfulness gives you tools to measure and manage your life as you're living it. It teaches you to pay attention to the present moment, recognize your thoughts and emotions and keep them under control, especially in highly stressful situations. When you are fully mindful, you're aware of your presence and the ways you impact other people. You're able to both observe your own thoughts and emotions and recognize the implications of your actions on others.

Cathy in the Jungle

When I was in Bermuda doing anthropological research, I had an opportunity to test my own observer-self skills while learning how to be accepted by a group of macaques. The experience was not without missteps. On one occasion, a playful young macaque snuck up from behind me and pulled my hair! Did I remain conscious and in the moment? No. Regrettably, I screamed, alerting all 20 of the macaques. I not only frightened the baby who had simply been curious about me, but I lost a week's worth of data that flew from my clipboard as I ran to safety. As unfortunate as this incident was, I learned that as an anthropologist, one must listen and expect risk as well as observe without judgment.

Practicing mindfulness and strengthening your observer-self will prevent you from slipping into a life that pulls you away from your values. We don't use the word "practice" lightly. In order to gain awareness and clarity about the present moment, you must be able to quiet your mind. With continued conscious effort, you will get better at it throughout your life. There are many ways you can work to improve mindfulness, and meditation is one of them.

Exercise: Beginning Mindful Meditation

- Find a quiet place with few distractions to allow for more focus and fewer interruptions. This can be particularly helpful for beginners.

- Meditation can be done while sitting, lying down, standing, walking or in any other position. Choose what is most comfortable for you and what allows you to focus without physical pain or discomfort, and without dozing off. If you are a beginner, it's best to not lie down because you will tend to fall asleep.

- Stopping the ever-present train of thoughts in the mind is much easier said than done. A good way to begin is to take several slow, deep breaths into your abdomen. Think about how your body breathes and notice what it feels like to have air go into your lungs and back out. Allow your muscles to relax from the neck down by consciously thinking about each area and relaxing it.

- Take notice of any thoughts you have and then let them go. Let them float into your mind and then float back out.

- Let your thoughts come and go as you remain positive and relaxed. Practice being grateful for the small as well as the big things that are a part of your life.

While many people including professionals are embracing meditation, it's not for everyone. The important thing is to have a set time each day to pull back from the pressures and reflect on what is happening. In addition to meditation, many take time for reflecting while walking, hiking or jogging among other physical activities. Regardless of the daily introspective practice you choose, the pursuit of mindfulness will help you achieve more clarity about what's important to you and a deeper understanding of the world around you.

TC's Mindful Training

For me, there is an activity that is even more powerful than meditation in developing my mindfulness (and I meditate almost daily). I roller ski for my workouts when there's good weather. Roller skiing is like cross- country skiing except on paved roads using inline skates and cross-country ski racing poles. I ski the neighborhood streets where I live. Since a small stone, stick or wet leaf can cause me to fall, I have to pay attention in the moment and focus on the road directly in front of me. But because I have skied over 10,000 miles, I can use a relaxed focus and allow my mind to drift. This approach quiets my thoughts and allows me to listen to what my mind and body wants in that workout. Some days, if I'm tired or tense, I ski slowly and use the workout to rejuvenate my mind and relax my body. Other days, when my energy is high, I might sprint up every hill.

Mindfulness… sip by sip

In the best-selling business book, , the authors suggest we live life "sip by sip" rather than "gulp by gulp" as most of us do. The book is written by Banana Republic founders Mel and Pat Ziegler and entrepreneur Bill Rosenzweig who developed their venture based on mindfulness. The authors propose that business has become the "dominant metaphor of our time" and that the powerful changes we want to make in this world will come through our enterprises. However, it won't be with the business practices we once knew. Instead, our work will be discernible by community service, authenticity, communication, personal growth, creativity and relationships.

You have to breathe, you are always thinking and you have an observer-self. So, learning to be mindful isn't really learning something new; it's learning how to be in more conscious control of what you are already doing.

SHARPEN YOUR FOCUS

Take some time to think about what you've learned and briefly summarize that knowledge here. When you've finished reading this book, these collected thoughts will provide you with a shot of "instant" inspiration as you apply these lessons to your life.

_____

_____

_____

_____

_____

Chapter Eight
Create Mindful Moments
and Mindfulness is Powerful

"The little things? The little moments? They aren't little."
                                                    -Jon Kabat-Zinn

A street musician, a violinist, stood at a Washington D.C. metro station early in the morning. He played about six pieces of Bach. It took around an hour for him to get through them and in that time, an estimated 2,000 people passed through the station. One gentleman in particular stopped for a moment to listen and then rushed off when his train arrived.

After four minutes more, the musician took notice of one dollar thrown in his tin by a woman who had barely stopped.

After six minutes, another man waiting stood against the wall to listen for a moment until he had to leave.

After ten minutes, a young boy, about 3-years-old, tried to stop and show his mother but she pushed him to keep walking. In fact, this happened with many of the children walking by. All of the parents urged their children to keep walking hurriedly.

After 45 minutes, the musician had collected $32 from about 20 people who just walked by, none of them really stopping to enjoy the music. About six people stayed to listen, but hadn't left money.

One hour in, he stopped playing. No one took notice.

What all of these people didn't know was that this violinist was one of the finest musicians in the world, named Joshua Bell. His violin was worth over $3.5 million dollars. It was only two days before when people had bought tickets at an average of $100 apiece for his sold out concert.

The Washington Post set up this social experiment to view the perception of beauty, taste and priorities. One of the biggest questions that stood out from this was how we recognize talent in an unexpected context. Their conclusion? "If we do not have a moment to stop and listen to one of the best musicians in the world, playing some of the finest music ever written, with one of the most beautiful instruments...how many other things are we missing?"

Do you create moments of mindfulness or is your mind on unconscious auto-response all day? The mindful moment is that instant that allows you to be absolutely and fully present in your most powerful, creative, knowledgeable and wise self. It is when you take your mind off auto-response and consciously gain control of your thoughts and emotions. The mindful moment is where mental magic happens. It's your best stuff. It's when your most creative solutions occur to you. Live in the mindful moment and create insights and wisdom. To live in the mindful moment, you must choose to live in the unknown. Being present and living in a mindful moment with no particular attachment to any thought will likely be uncomfortable until you get used to the peacefulness of it. And if you remember back to chapter 2 of this book, there is value in getting comfortable being uncomfortable.

Since being mindful is valuable, wouldn't it benefit you if you could increase the length and depth of your mindful moments, from milliseconds to a second, or to five minutes? The more of these mindful moments you have and the longer you can live in them, the more mindful you become. **Create mindful moments is the eighth Fearless Leaders' success secret.**

Exercise: Expand the Mindful Moment

- Think of a problem you are working on fixing.
- Apply all of the related information you have to resolve the problem.

- Evaluate as many solutions as you can, without judgment, on how well each might work. Notice all of your thoughts and emotions as you do.
- Deepen and slow your breathing and let yourself be introspective.
- Ask yourself these questions: What are all the possibilities? What would work for everyone? What's a creative solution that's not obvious?
- Breathe deeply and slowly.
- Take as much time as you choose.
- When you are ready, return your awareness to your current situation. If you haven't yet found the solution you are seeking, it's okay. By creating a deep, extended mindful moment you have engaged your subconscious mind; it will keep working on the solution, while your conscious mind takes on other tasks.

Exercise: Increase the Frequency of Mindful Moments

To increase how often you consciously create mindful moments, you can develop cues for yourself. Let's examine some of the different signals that indicate when it would be helpful to create a mindful moment.

Three Types of Mindful Moment Cues

1. Mental cues:
- Negative thoughts
- Fearful thoughts
- Angry thoughts
- Contradictory thoughts
- Limiting thoughts

2. Emotional cues:
- Stress
- Anxiety

- Fear
- Anger
- Confusion

3. Physical cues:
  - Your breathing is faster and more shallow
  - You have tension in your neck, chest, back or abdomen
  - Your stomach feels like it's churning
  - You are clenching your fists or jaw
  - The palms of your hands, forehead or armpits are sweating
  - Your face is reddening

Let's say you have chosen shallow breathing as your mindful moment cue. When you notice yourself breathing in your upper chest instead of into your abdomen, you can immediately create some mindfulness. In this moment you can decide to change your thinking and breathing, to evaluate all of your options on how to respond or react to what is taking place outside of you. By noticing your shallow breathing, you have engaged your observer-self, stayed off of auto-response and created more mindfulness for yourself.

Each time you create a mindful moment, it strengthens your ability to create other mindful moments. The more your brain fires the neurons that create a mindful moment, the stronger your mindful neural pathway becomes. Applying this secret is easy, but mastering it is a lifelong process. You just need to be very intentional in consciously creating a moment where you're paying attention on purpose, in the moment, without judgment. And, if you make a judgment about a thought that crosses your mind, just let it go.

Mindful Moments Can be Transcendent

When you master your mind to the level that you can consciously choose to have mindful moments, you create expanded possibilities and can then make higher conscious choices and decisions from these possibilities. When you are being mindful, you might even transcend rational thought and be able to engage with your own subconscious mind. For example, the founder and CEO of a high-tech firm shared with us: "I earn my paycheck about once a quarter, for an idea that I have, or a decision I make that significantly improves the company." He continued, "It is usually an idea that comes to me as I'm staring out the window or playing my guitar."

Mindfulness Saved TC's Life

I was 58-years-old when I enrolled in the Guapa Vista surfing camp in Jaco, Costa Rica. On the fourth day we took a break and visited Manuel Antonio National Park where we went on an amazing walking tour. At the end of the trail, we stopped to swim at the most serene beach I've ever seen. Everyone, including David and Luciana, went out to play in the calm ocean. David Segura was one of the surfing instructors at the camp. He had driven us to the park and had brought his girlfriend Luciana Komeroski with him. Luciana and I had been introduced, but she didn't speak English so we had not had a conversation.

For a while, I just sat on the beach soaking in the incredible scenery in every direction. We were in a cove and the surrounding hills were covered with trees. The waves were gentle and David, Luciana and the other folks from the surfing camp all seemed joyful.

The waves grew just enough while we were there that David and Luciana began to body surf. I've done quite a bit of body surfing and when I saw them, I made a beeline into the water. I felt completely safe in this very gentle surf and caught a wave that lifted me up and carried me all the way in to shore where it laid me down in a few inches of water. As the wave receded, it left me laying on the sand. It was the perfect body surfing ride.

The joy of that moment was envigorating and I ran back into the ocean with a smile that covered my whole face. I stopped where I had been catching waves in chest deep water. As I watched the next wave approach, I noticed it was breaking a little bit early, but so did the last wave and it had given me the perfect ride. Now with the breaker about eight feet from me, I began to swim as hard as I could toward shore in order to catch it.

Then I caught a glimpse of the wave and it had completely changed from being friendly and small to a much bigger one with white water driving straight down. I remember thinking, *it looks like it has fangs*, that's the last memory I have for the next three hours of my life.. That kind of wave is what surfers call a closer wave. Others may call it a rogue wave.

The wave drove me headfirst into the bottom of the ocean and left me floating facedown, unconscious. When David realized that the wave was changing and becoming a closer wave, he and Luciana dived underneath it. Fortunately, David is a mindful man. Without hesitation after surfacing, he looked up and down the beach to see if the closer wave had hurt anybody. He saw me floating face down about 50 yards away. He and Luciana ran through the water as fast as they could, turned me over and pulled me up onto the beach, still unconscious.

I regained some level of consciousness after a few minutes, but it wasn't until leaving the hospital three hours later that I could think clearly and answer questions coherently. I was badly hurt and felt alone and vulnerable.

For the hour and a half ride back to our surfing camp, Luciana endured the discomfort of sitting on the metal floor of the van so that she could comfort me. During the whole trip, she gently kept her hand on my left shoulder. She seemed to intuitively know exactly how I felt.

Both David and Luciana are masterfully mindful. Because of David's mindfulness, I'm alive and have no brain damage. He saved my physical life. Luciana revived me spiritually.

From the Depths of Mindfulness Comes Expanded Creativity

You have to allow yourself to be completely receptive within the moment of mindfulness to fully benefit. "Allowing" is the passive part of creativity and creation. Your intent is the active part. You must accept the paradox of having intent to be creative but not work at being creative. When you are mindful, you allow thoughts, ideas, images and feelings without judgment. Examples would be to develop a new strategy, solve a problem, resolve a conflict or create something new. Though you can't force answers, you can catalyze them by asking yourself quality questions.

Questions stimulate creativity. The better the questions you ask yourself, the better the answers you will receive. Instead of asking questions like, "What's wrong with this?" Ask yourself, "What are the possibilities here?" Another question could be, "How could this work for everyone?" Everyone, including not just you and your clients or the users of a product or service, but also family members. Dianne Collins in her enlightening book, *Do You Quantum Think?: New Thinking That Will Rock Your World,* goes into great depth on how to do this.

Got Willpower?

When you are on auto-response, willpower is not in play because you repeat what you always do. But when you create mindfulness, you also enable your willpower. Then when you lengthen and deepen your mindfulness, you lengthen and deepen your willpower. By doing so, you can create many choices for yourself on how to act, rather than having limited choices being on auto-response.

You can start to practice these choices at any age. The following describes a funny video called "The Marshmallow Experiment" in which Walter Michel at Stanford University conducted an experiment on delayed gratification and willpower.

In this study, a group of four-year-old children were each given a marshmallow. They had a choice to either eat it right away or wait and get a second one when the researcher returned. Some children could wait, while others couldn't. The researchers then followed each child into adolescence, revealing that those with the ability to wait were actually better adjusted and more determined. They also scored an average of 210 points higher on the Scholastic Aptitude Test.

Nelson Mandela

Nelson Mandela evolved over his lifetime to become one of the most mentally tough, mindful leaders in history. He led the anti-apartheid movement, which was responsible for the emancipation of South Africa from white minority rule, and then served as his country's first black president. He was known for his forbearance, forgiveness and mindfulness.

Most people being oppressed and denigrated like he was would end up filled with hatred and possibly seek vengeance. How did Mandela overcome his anger and hatred of his oppressors and captors who had humiliated him and his people, tortured and murdered many of his friends, and put him in prison for 27 years?

When a question like this was posed to Mandela in an interview he said, "Hating clouds the mind. It gets in the way of strategy. Leaders cannot afford to hate." Hating is a judgment and Mandela had become so mindful that he had freed himself of these destructive judgments and emotions to create solutions others could not. He had learned to be a master of his mind and became powerful by doing so. **This is the ninth Fearless Leaders' secret, mindfulness is powerful.**

Creating Mindful Moments During a Disagreement

When you live mindful moments more often and for longer periods of time, you also minimize the number of conflicts you have and improve your relationships. On a personal level, could you create a mindful moment if your teenage son or daughter came to you and told you about friends who were using drugs? But if your children know that you are highly reactive, then they'll likely never talk with you about sensitive topics like this.

Or professionally, if team members or colleagues have a different perspective but know that you tend to react defensively when disagreed with, do you think they will openly express their opinions?

You can consciously create more powerful mindfulness when someone disagrees with your perspective. Immediately after you realize you are in disagreement with another person there is an enormous opportunity to expand your thinking by truly listening to and learning from them.

When someone offers a different viewpoint, rather than defending your position, consider saying, "That's interesting." This is a neutral response. You are neither agreeing nor disagreeing, but you are building a positive rapport with the person you are talking with as well as enriching your knowledge.

Cathy Keeps Her Cool Under Duress

I was tested at creating mindful moments in a three-day program led by Bill Filter and Bill Kipp along with Mark Williams, retired major and former F-15C pilot at the 58th Tactical Fighter Squadron. Major Williams has trained world-class athletes, firefighters, police and SWAT officers, U.S. Special Forces, Norwegian fighter pilots and more. This program, through their organization Dynamic Human Solutions (www.dynamichumansolutions.com), was customized to each individual seeking to excel at command presence in the face of danger.

I learned to use a breathing technique to control my mind and body so I could prevail in verbal confrontations and even physical assaults. The idea was to train the brain, train the voice and learn appropriate actions and reactions. If you let fear prevail, an assailant will continue to move against you in a verbal confrontation. People will use a verbal confrontation like a shark might bump into you in the water. They want to see what kind of reaction they will get from you. If they sense fear, they know they have a vulnerable target.

For me, the program was one of the best experiences I've had. It helped me develop mindfulness even under the extreme stress of being attacked.

Winning Hearts and Minds

During the war in Iraq, many villages around Fallujah were surviving as a result of the established authority of terrorists with networks who provided protection, food and a pipeline that supported the existing populations. The mindset of the local population was aligned to "protect" what they had come to know and trust.

When U.S. forces infiltrated this area, one of the biggest issues became the need for immediate medical attention for Iraqi civilians. In particular, the children were among the most deeply impacted by injury, infection and disease. The U.S. military on the ground committed to helping by setting up basic life support hospitals. Iraqi's grew to appreciate and trust the American troops as a result. The vision of soldiers carrying wounded and dying Iraqi children to their makeshift medical facilities was powerful. Helping these children was both the right humanitarian and political decision. It was also a mindful deed that helped turn the tide against the resident insurgents.

Exercise: Expand Mindfulness in a Disagreement

Both in your professional and personal relationships there will be lots of occasions when people will disagree with you. Here are some steps for learning to create mindful moments in these situations:

- Imagine someone disagreeing with you.
- Instead of arguing or defending your position, drop your thoughts into a mindful moment and respond with, "That's interesting."
- Then say, "I'd like to understand why you think that."
- Listen without judgment. Focus only on deeply understanding the other person's perspective.

Repeat the above steps many times using different people and scenarios to build this new neural pathway. A few examples to get you started are:

- An occasion when you feel that a project should move ahead while a colleague thinks that it should be tabled

- A heated discussion with your teenager about using the family car
- A relaxing dinner out with your loved ones during which family budget issues come under discussion

Preventing the Limbic Loop

Another powerful benefit of developing your mindfulness is to prevent the limbic loop. The essence of the limbic loop is that each time a thought goes through the limbic (emotional) part of your brain, it recruits exponentially more neurons, thus increasing the intensity of your emotion. It doesn't take too many loops through the limbic system before the emotional reaction is so strong that it can't be stopped. Think of a time when an emotion like anger, sadness or even joy took complete control of your brain and you couldn't stop it. This is the limbic loop.

You may have also heard this referred to as the "amygdala hijack." The amygdala hijack is a term coined by Daniel Goleman in his 1996 book *Emotional Intelligence: Why It Can Matter More Than IQ*. Drawing on the work of Joseph E. LeDoux, Goleman uses the term to describe emotional responses from people which are immediate and overwhelming, and out of measure with the actual stimulus.

The best way to curtail this is to be mindful in between a stimulus and your first thoughts about it. Or be able to use the four-step thought replacement technique discussed earlier to thwart a destructive thought before it makes many loops.

SHARPEN YOUR FOCUS

Take some time to think about what you've learned and briefly summarize that knowledge here. When you've finished reading this book, these collected thoughts will provide you with a shot of "instant" inspiration as you apply these lessons to your life.

_____

_____

_____

_____

_____

Chapter Nine
Climb the Consciousness
Mountain

"Consciousness is contagious."
-Sigmund Freud

Your consciousness influences everyone around you. Have you ever spent time with a self-centered person only looking out for himself, or a joyous person who always looks out for the greater good of all? If you have, you know firsthand how that person's consciousness affected you. There are infinite levels of conscious awareness. While all levels are available for you to live in, you actually function at many levels simultaneously with varying degrees throughout your life. So there is not one singular level you live at. You are instead a work in progress managing with what you have as best as you can. Which means those who are among the best in the world at what they do, whether it's business, sports, military special operations or humanitarianism, don't think of others as the competition. They know the only real competition is themselves.

Increasing your consciousness then is like climbing your own inner mountain. You can see more and perceive more as you go higher. The bigger your perspective, the greater number of possibilities you have or can create. **The tenth Fearless Leaders' success secret is climb the consciousness mountain.**

Definitions of consciousness

Consciousness refers to being aware of your unique thoughts, memories, emotions, sensations and environment. Your conscious experiences are constantly shifting and changing. For example, in one moment, you may be focused on reading this book and in the next that you are thirsty. There are two primary degrees of consciousness as represented by the continuum below:

Lower consciousness .... Higher consciousness

- **Lower consciousness** involves thoughts mostly concerned with survival of the self and/or those closest to you. Your lower conscious thoughts are primarily involved with the four F's: Fighting, Fleeing, Feeding and Fornicating.
- **Higher consciousness** applies when you transcend your own experiences and extend yourself and your understanding to encompass humanity's highest potential such as how your thoughts and actions affect all life on Earth.

Cathy's Understanding about Being Human

In a project for the Pentagon I worked with a group of high-ranking flag officers (flag officers are mostly generals and admirals). I was asked to develop "coaching modules" on subjects that ranged from "Ethics" to "Operating At the Edge." These topics would undoubtedly make the difference in the lives of millions of people under the command of these officers. Upon final project review, I was told that the material was very good and would be edited and applied but, it was too "soft."

I replied with something like this, "In many years of working with executives, CEO's, boards, military professionals including our highest ranking officers and government officials, they have said with great clarity—'anyone can teach us the skills to be better strategic leaders, what we need is to **learn how to be better human beings with a higher consciousness and moral courage, so we can be**

better leaders.'" To be a better, more Fearless Leader, you need to continue to become a more evolved human being.

The Triple Bottom Line

This phrase was first coined in 1994 by John Elkington, the founder of a British consulting firm called SustainAbility. His premise was that companies should be preparing three different, and quite separate, bottom lines. One is the traditional measure of a company's financial profit—the financial bottom line. The second is of the company's "people account"—a measure in some shape or form of how it treats all the people who interact in any way with the organization. The third is the company's "planet account"—a measure of how environmentally responsible it has been. The Triple Bottom Line thus consists of three Ps: Profit, People and Planet. It aims to measure the financial, social and environmental performance of the corporation over a period of time. Companies that pay attention to a triple bottom line are doing business with a higher consciousness.

Whole Foods

When we are fully aware of our thoughts, emotions and actions and how they affect everyone and everything, we are using higher consciousness. John Mackey, co-CEO of Whole Foods, practices a higher level of consciousness in his company. He shares these concepts with us in his book *Conscious Capitalism*. Mackey believes that business can be "good" for society by merging awareness and capitalism. Whole Foods continues to become more conscious and has grown into a powerful company. The success of Whole Foods is an excellent example of the benefits of mindful, higher consciousness thinking.

The Importance of Decision-Making

Napoleon Hill studied over 25,000 people who had experienced failure and concluded that a lack of effective decision-making was one of the top causes of the setbacks these people had experienced.

When you have an important decision to make should you base it on logic, follow your heart or make an intuitive choice? According to Warren Bennis, an American scholar, organizational consultant, author and widely regarded as a pioneer in the contemporary field of leadership studies, leaders affect the lives of innumerable people so it's vital they have great decision-making processes that allow them to implement higher conscious choices.

He also stated that one of the best speeches ever given was by Martin Luther King, Jr. in 1963, reminding us that it is in times of crisis that any intervention has more impact than in times of stability.

But, what makes one a leader? In previous writings, Bennis questioned, like most of us, why certain people seem to naturally inspire confidence and loyalty while others hesitate and stagger. While there may not be a single answer, most can agree that it has something to do with how people deal with misfortune and hardship. True leadership comes from ones' ability to make meaning out of adversity and negative circumstance. A Fearless Leader has mastered the skill to conquer difficulty and come out stronger and more dedicated.

Bennis also identified one of the most impactful and difficult decisions ever made was by Harry Truman, the 33rd president of the United States. He was faced with whether to use atomic bombs on Hiroshima and Nagasaki that would end World War II, but at an enormous cost to innocent people in Japan.

Harry Truman's Three-step Decision-Making Process

Truman used a well-defined three-step process and essentially made a logical, an emotional and then an intuitive decision. He was very clear on the importance of going through each of the first two steps completely before the third. No shortcuts! Here are the steps:

1. **The logical decision.** Gather the best information from people who know the most about the subject. To end with a great decision, you must begin with great information. Make a pro and con list and determine your logical decision.

2. **The emotional decision.** Search your heart for your emotional decision. Truman's emotional decision was to **not** drop the bomb. He hated the idea of hurting innocent people for years to come from the radiation. Your emotional decision is often very forthright, so don't confuse it with your intuitive decision which is often very quiet.

3. **The intuitive decision.** In this third step, you need to get away from thinking consciously about your decision. You need to allow your subconscious mind an opportunity to pull all the information together at a level below your consciousness, then pay attention to your intuition. You may find your intuitive message in the pit of your stomach, like Harry Truman did, or it could be a quiet sense of knowing. It's different for everyone.

Notice that the third step of Harry Truman's decision-making process was living in the mindful moment. The logical decision examines past and future. The emotional decision is based on an attachment to an experience also based on the past and the future. The mindful moment is the integration of all the logical and emotional information and experiences in a way you might not be able to fully express. Your most profound challenges, even the ones that seem impossible, are often answered by being still in the mindful moment.

A Better Safer World

We seek leaders with a higher consciousness because we want to follow those who can think and act towards the greater good of all. Regardless of religion, culture, heritage, there is one thing we all want. We want a better world for our children and we believe leaders with a higher consciousness will help make it one. Increasing consciousness worldwide can happen fairly quickly. Andrew Shi, from the University of California, Davis has studied consciousness in a variety of groups. "In almost every species we have looked at, we find individuals are consistently different in their behaviors over time and across situations. Therefore—they learn, adapt and even pass these qualities along to those around them, especially their off-spring. Thus, there is the ability to evolve a new level of 'consciousness' called a behavioral 'adaptation' or a behavioral way of being in as little as one generation or within the lifetime of that animal species."

This means when you lift your own consciousness, you can have a consciousness raising influence on everyone around you.

Exercise: Levels of a Conscious Decision

- What is a challenging question or situation where you need to make a decision on what to do?
- Take a moment to deepen and slow your breathing and thoughts. Become mindful of your options.
- Think of as many different decisions you can come up with that could solve your challenge. Include the lowest and highest consciousness choices as well as everything in the middle.

SHARPEN YOUR FOCUS

Take some time to think about what you've learned and briefly summarize that knowledge here. When you've finished reading this book, these collected thoughts will provide you with a shot of "instant" inspiration as you apply these lessons to your life.

_____

_____

_____

_____

_____

SECTION IV:
EXCEL WITH UNRELENTING FIRE

CHAPTER TEN
PASSION IS THE FUEL OF GREATNESS

"There is no passion to be found playing small—in settling
for a life that is less than the one you're capable of living."
–Nelson Mandela

You can be good, maybe even very good, at what you do without
tremendous passion for it. But to be great you must have unrelenting fire. **Passion is the fuel of greatness is the eleventh Fearless
Leaders' success secret.**

Definition of Passion

Passion is an intense emotion, a compelling feeling or desire for
something. It's a drive of unusual excitement or enthusiasm, a positive affinity or love, towards something or someone. Passion is literally a form of falling in love. The biochemical changes that occur in
your brain when you have great passion for your life's purpose or a
specific goal is the same as when you fall in love.

Jim Collins wrote in his book, *Good to Great*, "The good-to-great
companies focused on those activities that ignited their passions.
The idea here is not to stimulate passion but to discover what makes
you passionate."

In another book by Jim Collins, *Great by Choice*, he writes that
fanatic discipline is one of the characteristics of the great by choice
companies and their leaders. Discipline can mean different things
to different people. The discipline Collins and his team found in

the best-performing leaders was consistency of action—consistency with values, long-term goals and performance standards; consistency of method; and consistency over time. It involves rejecting conventional wisdom, hype and the madness of crowds—and instead essentially to be a nonconformist. An example of one of Collins' fanatically disciplined leaders, John Brown of Stryker, had the long-term goal of 20 percent annual net income growth every year and he achieved this mark more than 90 percent of the time over the 21 years he targeted.

In *Judgment: How Winning Leaders Make Great Calls* by Noel Tichy and Warren Bennis, the authors emphasize that good judgement is central to leadership. Nobody is always right, however top leaders consistently show good judgement. Tichy and Bennis break down the process of making tough decisions by showing how to recognize the signs that a decision will need to be forthcoming, when that decisive action is to take place and how to execute on that decision. Noel Tichy and Chris DeRose followed up with a more indepth book in 2013, *Judgment on the Front Line: How Smart Companies Win By Trusting Their People,* which shows that even hourly employees on the front line need the skills and decision-making capability to truly embrace the passion they have for doing their best.

Having unrelenting passion makes self-discipline and organizational discipline so much easier. This is crucial not only for yourself, but also for those with whom you form partnerships, either personal or professional.

We have found one of the distinguishing traits of passionate, high-performing organizations is an obsessive focus by the people in it on both the *what* and *how*. The *what* in business is the one thing the business is known for. What product or service differentiates the company from others in its market? The *how* is creating a high-performance culture to sustain passion and great products or services.

So what's the one thing that you choose to be highly passionate about? For Alvaro Solano Delgado, the seven-time Costa Rican surfing champion who is now president of Vista Guapa Surf Camp, his one thing is surfing. He was not only passionate about competing as a surfer, but he is now a passionate instructor. He's like a proud parent watching his child take her first steps each time a student new to surfing catches that first wave.

When his students, who are mostly tourists, get tired and need a break, Alvaro takes that time to teach the local kids at the beach how to surf for free until his students are ready to go out again. When asked why he taught these kids for free he replied, "They are Costa Ricans and I want them to love the ocean and surfing the way I do." Alvaro also has fear combined with his passion. What is he afraid of? Without hesitation he said succinctly, "Drowning!" He has accepted that possibility but it does not deter him from living his passion.

A Mindful Moment Followed by Unrelenting Fire

Why do you think millions of girls miss school and women miss work in Third World countries? One surprising answer was discovered by Elizabeth Scharpf in Mozambique in 2005 while studying how small and medium-sized businesses can play a role in developing economies. One day she overheard a local colleague's concern that her women employees often didn't come into work because they were menstruating. Hearing this, Scharpf apparently had a mindful moment and decided to look into the situation further.

First, she learned why the education of girls was so critical to these countries. A study fielded by the Council on Foreign Relations, "Addressing the Special Needs of Girls," found that each additional year of secondary education increased a woman's potential earnings by about 25 percent.

Another study found that 18 percent of school age girls in Rwanda missed school because menstrual pads are too expensive. In countries like Mozambique and Rwanda, where the per capita standard of living is under $1,000 per year, the average annual cost of the cheapest sanitary pads was $33 a year, making them unaffordable. Because menstruation was a taboo subject, no one had ever considered addressing the problem.

One of the most basic premises of entrepreneurial thinking is to find a need in the market and provide a cost-effective solution. This case presented both a business and humanitarian need. But instead of simply raising charity to import finished pads, Scharpf and the organization she founded, Sustainable Health Enterprises (SHE), created a franchise model to partner with women in Rwanda and other developing country communities to market their own SHE franchises. As product is sold, some of the initial working capital that SHE invests is paid back, with the entrepreneurs eventually owning their local franchises. The cycle continues as SHE reinvests its profits in new geographies or other enterprises to empower many impassioned women franchise owners.

Scharpf is a mindful disruptor, like most of the leaders whose stories we share with you in this book. She got to see in herself and others what really inspires passion. Hers was to improve lives. She also realized this passion is good for business. She is not alone in this realization as more and more people are also recognizing it to be true. Gretchen Spreitzer and Christine Porath reported in a recent issue of *Harvard Business Review* that for organizations to prosper today, their employees need to feel as if they are "engaged in creating the future—the company's and their own."

Consider David Farr, CEO of Emerson Electric, who is noted for asking virtually everyone he encounters in his organization at least these three questions related to his company's story:

1. How do you make a difference? (testing for alignment with the company's direction)
2. What improvement idea are you working on? (emphasizing continuous improvement)
3. When did you last get coaching from your boss? (emphasizing the importance of employee development)

Cathy on Leadership Across Tiers

When working with a global pharmaceutical organization, we brought together team leaders from regional groups around the world, then they met with a larger group of senior executives to share their success stories and learn from each other's regional experiences. Those success stories and regional experiences were then shared throughout the organization personally in working groups, webinars and other media. As a result, the entire supporting functions of the organization and especially the senior executive team became more aligned and committed to the contributions that each region was making to their overall global success.

All of this may beg the question of who is actually in charge and why do the opinions of lower echelon employees matter? Noel Tichy addresses this in his hallmark theory about maintaining a "Teachable Point of View." In what he calls a "virtuous teaching cycle," setting the stage for mutual learning requires that the teachers be open to learning themselves and that the learners have the self-confidence to absorb their instructors' knowledge and then to develop their own ability to teach. All of this should take place in a non-hierarchical environment.

Unfortunately, as management experts Tichy and Chris DeRose explain, most organizations don't know how to evaluate the risk of giving employees more autonomy. Many of those who are willing to try haven't even invested resources in ensuring once the shackles are off that the front-line employees make good judgments. Tichy and DeRose offer powerful examples of front line leadership, such as how Zappos trusts its people to do anything in service of a customer, including providing free product or reimbursing for mistakes and how the Mayo Clinic of Arizona enables its nurses to challenge the hierarchy in order to improve patient care.

Many executives are surprised not only by the ownership and drive for implementation that comes from high-involvement approaches, but also by the improved quality of the answers that emerge as noted in Tichy's book, *On the Front Line*. Also, in speaking to *Harvard Business Review* in November 2008, John Chambers, chairman and CEO of networking specialist Cisco Systems, described his experience this way, "It was hard for me at first to learn to be collaborative. The minute I'd get into a meeting, I'd listen for about ten minutes while the team discussed a problem. I knew what the answer was, and eventually I'd say, 'All right, here's what we're going to do.' But when I learned to let go and give the team the time to come to the right conclusion, I found they made just as good decisions, or even better—and just as important, they were even more invested in the decision and thus executed with greater speed and commitment."

What it comes down to, of course, is that when people make their own decisions, they are more dedicated to everything that follows.

TC Tells of the Unrelenting Fire of an Impoverished Boy
Because he had no parents, a destitute orphan in Africa was raised by his older brother. He didn't even have a pair of shoes, but he was a talented endurance runner and decided he would race his way out of poverty. One day, he made a promise to his older brother. He said, "I will become a world champion, move out of this country and never live in poverty again." A bold statement for sure.

But this boy ran every day. He developed his raw talent and did indeed live up to the promise he made to his brother by becoming a world champion. He also attended college on an athletic scholarship and has become a successful businessman.

I had the pleasure of working with this athlete after he won his world championship. He was training better and faster than ever. But he said, "I've lost the fire. It's not there like it used to be when I need it now." In a long race, when his body began to give out, when his muscles were depleted, he no longer had the reserve of energy he had before when he became a world champion. It was his passion that previously would kick in and allow him to finish his race strong. It had been there from the time he made that commitment to his brother until he had achieved his goal of winning the world championship. His passion was to become a world champion and to lift himself out of poverty. Once accomplished, no other goal inspired the unrelenting fire.

Americans Are Unhappy in Their Jobs

Americans are quitting their jobs because they are seeking more personal fulfillment in their lives. Several recent studies confirm that employee turnover rates are on the rise. A Kelly Services survey reports that 44 percent of the global workforce feels valued by their employer while 66 percent intend to look for a new job with another organization in the next year. The survey also concludes that 74 percent of those who are content with their current employment are seeking greater engagement from their positions and cite the ability to "excel or develop" as the key to providing a sense of meaning, personal and professional growth, a sense of purpose and more spiritual experience in their work.

In her book, *Kensho: A Modern Awakening,* Susan Steinbrecher examines why Americans are so disgruntled with their work. She believes that today many are challenging their beliefs and the frameworks they have constructed for their lives. They're yearning for more meaningful connections, more purpose in every aspect of life, to do something that has significance and value, something through which they can make a difference in the world. "What's really important?" is a question many are asking. More and more people have become disenchanted particularly with corporate life as it exists. Many feel trapped and unappreciated.

Steinbrecher says it well in a *Harvard Business Review* blog: "In this era of transition, company leadership must cultivate workplace happiness and provide a sense of meaning and engagement for employees that nourishes the human spirit.

"I encourage managers to connect with the emotional needs of employees and find ways to promote productivity while fostering creativity, meaning and fulfillment. Equally important is the self-awareness of company leadership. Over 70 percent of leaders fail or derail in their careers because they lack interpersonal skills. Being a good leader means pushing and expanding your own personal limits, and having the integrity and motivation to take the time to focus internally."

CEO of Miraval, Michael Tompkins, is one of those good leaders and co-author of the award-winning book, *Mindful Living* based on the famous program by the same name. *Mindful Living* is designed to help you more fully celebrate each moment of your life. Twelve specialists from the Miraval resort—ranging from exercise physiologists to chefs to spiritual healers—bring their expertise to chapters centered on the key tenets of the Miraval philosophy, such as balance, joy and developing the ability to overcome obstacles. While the topics addressed in *Mindful Living* may seem broad, they are held together through the concept of mindfulness, passion and purpose.

Passion and Purpose

Nobody can tell you what your purpose is, but once you have found it, you will be inspired to take action. Obstacles that loom large can disappear. You can live in your most courageous self and realize your personal mission.

What's Your One Thing?

Individually, each of us needs to figure out: what's my one thing? Steven R. Covey, author of *T*, has stated, "The main thing is to keep the main thing the main thing." When we do and choose to pursue our purpose, life becomes simpler, less confusing and more focused on the path to high performance. In his many years of work with Covey, Steve Shallenberger was a key leader who helped build the world-renowned Covey Leadership Center. He led a stalwart team and built the time management division from a few training sessions to over 600 formal seminars in just one year. Inspired by his friend Covey, Steve and his son Rob launched a leadership and personal development company called Becoming Your Best.

Prior to taking on his current role as a leadership management consultant, Rob served as an officer and fighter pilot in the United States Air Force for more than 11 years. He was one of the top F-16 pilots and later was an instructor and mentor to young fighter pilots. Rob is able to leverage the many lessons he learned as a fighter pilot to help businesses succeed at every level with passion and purpose.

Passion Fuels Fearless Leaders

Sergeant David M. Gerardi. It's unusual for a member of the National Guard to receive a Silver Star for actions performed as a marine, but Sergeant Gerardi did following his actions in Afghanistan in 2011. Pinned down by enemy fire along with the rest of his unit, he demonstrated "stalwart determination and vigilance" by placing himself in harm's way while providing suppressive fire to allow the extraction of a wounded Afghan soldier. When interviewed, Gerardi's parents confirmed his utter and complete passion for the military, passion that both drove and inspired him to put himself at risk. Corporal Josh Davenport, who served with Gerardi, said that, "one of the biggest things we take from him is his heart. He puts everything into it."

Sheryl Sandberg. Not content with her own stellar accomplishments, Facebook's COO Sheryl Sandberg has brought her passion for equality to bear on the success, or lack thereof, of women in the corporate world. Speaking about her bestselling book, *Lean In: Women, Work and the Will to Lead,* Sandberg says that "we can change the power structure of our world...Each individual's success can make success a little easier for the next…In the future, there will be no female leaders. There will just be leaders."

Jeremy Bloom. When speaking with Bloom, it was apparent he had an inordinate amount of focus and passion for each of his ventures, initially freestyle skiing and football and now building two entrepreneurial organizations, his nonprofit, Wish of a Lifetime, and his international marketing company, Integrate. He said, "I went to Wharton when I was playing football for the Eagles…that's where I developed my passion for business. I was really considering real estate development but I didn't like the idea of limiting myself to bricks and mortars. I didn't like the limitations of that model."

Passion Overcomes Fear

Karl Mecklenburg articulated how he mastered his fear and stayed extraordinarily focused using his passion. He stated: "I wanted to be the greatest football player that ever played the game. I had no business thinking that—but that was my mission. I was expecting setbacks, knowing that it was an extravagant dream, but there wasn't anything that was going to get in the way." Passion strengthens courage and helps you blast through the obstacles that stop others. When you have more passion than fear, passion wins as Mecklenburg's did.

Rebecca Lolosoli is one of the most passionate of the Fearless Leaders included in this book. Humanitarians are often greatly passionate and she is more fervent about her cause than most. Her humanitarian mission to improve women's rights in Kenya is so strong that she has endured severe beatings and risked her life. She provides another great example of passion defeating fear even under great degrees of stress.

Exercise: Your Impassioned WHY

• Write a goal that is both important and risky for you.

_____

_____

_____

_____

- Now, write the reason why you want to accomplish your goal. How much passion is in your "Why"?

_____

_____

_____

_____

Five Steps to Finding Your Passion

Finding your passion means that you'll need to search deep within yourself. First, for what you're passionate about and then for what skills and competencies you possess that will serve this passion. Then match these against opportunities in the marketplace, refining your search by those opportunities with the best potential return or outcome.

1. Relax and take your time to think about everything that you are passionate about. It may help you to take this passion test: www. thepassiontest.com.

2. If you have not taken the passion test, then on a scale from zero to ten with zero being no passion and ten being complete passion, give a score to each item on your list.

3. If none of your items is at least an eight to ten, repeat steps one and two. If you have one or more items in which your passion level is eight or above, then come up with a list of skills and competencies you already have that apply. Also, add to this list skills and competencies you can easily learn that apply.

4. Now, turn your focus externally and think about the market. What jobs, careers or entrepreneurial ventures are possibilities that fit both your passion and your competencies? Do this market evaluation for each of your high passion areas in which you have significant skills and competencies.

5. Create a mindful moment. Allow thoughts and emotions to drift into your mind, notice them all. Which have the greatest pull for you?

SHARPEN YOUR FOCUS

Take some time to think about what you've learned and briefly summarize that knowledge here. When you've finished reading this book, these collected thoughts will provide you with a shot of "instant" inspiration as you apply these lessons to your life.

_____

_____

_____

_____

_____

CHAPTER ELEVEN
THE IMPOSSIBLE IS POSSIBLE

"In a time of crisis we all have the potential
to morph up to a new level
and do things we never thought possible."
-Stuart Wilde, author and researcher on consciousness

To make great decisions, or to expand their creativity, Fearless Leaders learn to be passionate **and** have a tranquil, expanded mind. It's in these mindful moments that creative solutions emerge.

When passion and mindfulness intersect...sometimes what seems impossible, becomes possible. As Audrey Hepbrun said, "Nothing is Impossible, the word itself says I'M POSSIBLE." **The impossible is possible is the twelfth Fearless Leaders' success secret.**

TC's Two-week Turnaround of a Professional Sports Team
The head coach of a professional soccer team that was in a horrible slump asked for help. His request: "We have two weeks to turn this team around to have a shot at the playoffs. What can you do?"

My initial thought was *probably nothing—there wasn't enough time.* Anyone who had worked with a professional sports team would probably say it's impossible to turn a slump around in two weeks by an outside consultant. But the challenge was intriguing, so I told the coach, "I don't know if we can do anything, but we'll spend some time with your players and staff to see what we might be able to do."

We soon discovered that although there seemed to be a good sense of camaraderie among the players, there was also a palpable, collective negativity just below the surface. We even asked the players what they thought might be the cause of their slump. But they didn't trust us and didn't have much to say in response.

So it seemed nothing would work within the time frame we had. This was one of those moments where, in order to possibly find a creative solution, we would have to let go of everything we believed about improving this team. We did, and consciously sat still being mindful for quite some time contemplating the situation, which was:

- We now had a week to identify and remedy what was causing this team to slump.
- The players didn't know us and we didn't have time to develop trusting relationships with them.
- There seemed to be good camaraderie and trust between the players.
- The players were resolved to be their best.
- Soccer was not only something they loved, it was also the job that fed their families.
- The players had a palpable negativity towards the coaches that no one would talk about.

In a flash of creativity, which in this case seemed more like a euphemism for desperation, a possible solution emerged. What if we could identify which of the players were most respected and trusted on the team and then work with those leaders as liaisons to the rest of the team? When we asked the players who they most trusted on the team, almost everyone gave us the same five names. Once identified, we asked these five leaders, "If we could guarantee no repercussions and that no specific players would be identified to the management in bringing up issues, would you work with us in a full team meeting without the coaches present?" They agreed.

The team members opened up quickly, identified several major concerns that had caused them to feel extremely resentful towards the coaches resulting in underperforming on the field. Next, with the permission of all the athletes, we met with the coaches in a separate room and outlined the team's issues. The coaches were surprised by what they heard, but were absolutely willing to make the requested changes.

The coaches joined the players and apologized for what they had unintentionally done to create the situation. The coaches then made specific commitments to resolve the issues and followed-through.

At the very next practice, there was a noticeable difference in the positive energy and physical effort of the team. From that day on, the team had great practices and played better in games. The two-week turnaround was a success—they made the playoffs!

A Positive Deviant Story

Jerry and Monique Sternin were on staff with Save the Children. The Vietnamese government asked them to help fight malnutrition amongst children throughout Vietnam's villages and gave the Sternins six months to make a difference. And if they didn't, they were done. If you were in the Sternin's place, what would you do?

Solving malnutrition for a whole country in six months with negligible resources was a seemingly impossible task. The conventional thinking to solve malnutrition was they had to address sanitation, ignorance, food distribution, poverty, disease and a lack of access to good water. But the Sternins were mindful and thought beyond convention for a solution. When they arrived in Vietnam, they adopted a beginner's attitude instead. They assumed they didn't have the answer and needed to listen, not talk.

They eventually turned to the theory of amplifying positive deviance. A positive deviant is an individual or group that is uncommonly successful compared with their peers when facing the same challenge and having the same resources.

The Sternins and others identified the positive deviants in four villages. The positive deviants were the families whose children were not malnourished. To understand what was positive deviant behavior, they had to determine the typical behavior of feeding the children.

They learned conventional Vietnamese wisdom was that certain foods were considered low-class, or common food, and parents didn't encourage eating them even though they were high in nutritional value.

They also discovered that most people were too busy working to take time to feed their children and they just left food out to be eaten. The children might eat it or might not. Some only fed their children once or twice a day.

The positive deviants, however, fed their children small amounts of food many times a day. These parents went to rice paddies and collected tiny shrimp and crabs to mix with their rice. They also included sweet potato greens with the rice, which by convention though was considered a low-class food. So the positive deviant parents were providing a meal that had carbohydrates (rice), protein (shrimp and crabs) and vitamins (sweet potato greens). Whereas the typical parent would just provide rice.

The next step was to make sure the practices of the positive deviants were self-sustaining and would spread without the Sternin's involvement. In Vietnam, for example, a health volunteer would invite eight to ten mothers into her home for training. As a price of entry, the mothers were required to bring a contribution of shrimp, crabs and sweet potato greens. The volunteers and mothers would then use those ingredients, along with rice, to cook a meal for the entire group. After two weeks of this, the training was over.

Most of the group would continue to gather shrimp and greens, and their children would continue to recover. Those families whose children didn't rehabilitate could re-enroll and go through the two-week process again, over and over, until the nutrition program became habitual.

In a two-year period, malnutrition dropped by 65 percent to 85 percent in the villages where the Sternins initially taught the behaviors of the positive deviant parents. But that's not the only amazing result: the Harvard School of Public Health visited the four original villages and did an independent study. They found that children who hadn't even been born when the Sternins left the villages were at the exact same enhanced nutritional levels as the ones who benefited from the program when they were there. This indicated that the behaviors were sustainable.

The Sternins took their positive deviance program to a total of 14 Vietnamese villages after succeeding in the initial four communities. As the program grew, it uncovered new solutions in new localities—for example, sesame seeds, peanuts and snails. The answers were never quite the same. Different solutions grew out of different soils. But the process remained the same. Discover original local answers to the problem and then give everyone access to the information.

The groundbreaking work that the Sternins did in Vietnam has served as a model for rehabilitating tens of thousands of children in 20 countries.

The successes of the people included in this chapter and throughout this book often seemed impossible. But when you combine the passion of unrelenting fire with mindful moments, the impossible sometimes becomes possible.

SHARPEN YOUR FOCUS

Take some time to think about what you've learned and briefly summarize that knowledge here. When you've finished reading this book, these collected thoughts will provide you with a shot of "instant" inspiration as you apply these lessons to your life.

CONCLUSION
YOU ARE A FEARLESS LEADER

"If your actions inspire others to dream more,
learn more, do more, and become more,
you are a leader."
- John Quincy Adams

The 12 Fearless Leaders' Success Secrets

1. Have the Courage to Fail In Order to Succeed
2. Get Comfortable Being Uncomfortable
3. Own It: No Blaming, Complaining or Excuses
4. Show Up Ready!
5. Be a Master of Mind Control
6. Value Critical Review
7. Think with Mindfulness
8. Create Mindful Moments
9. Mindfulness is Powerful
10. Climb the Consciousness Mountain
11. Passion is the Fuel of Greatness
12. The Impossible is Possible

We hope after reading all of the Fearless Leaders' stories, working on the exercises, and learning the 12 Fearless Leaders' success secrets, you understand that you too are already an evolving Fearless Leader.

You don't need to master all of the 12 Fearless Leaders' success secrets. It's a very rare person who has mastered all 12. The Fearless

Leaders in this book have all mastered at least one success secret though and are strong on many or all of the others. You can do it as well! Just make the decision to master one success secret, develop a plan and stay disciplined in implementing your plan.

In this last section we will briefly review the 12 success secrets and encourage you to select one to master beginning now and to select which ones you would like to work on strengthening. As you review each of the Fearless Leaders' success secrets, rate their importance in your life on a zero to ten scale where zero is of no value to you and ten indicates it's an absolute must for you to attain in order to get what you want. This will allow you to prioritize the success secret you want to focus on mastering and those you want to strengthen.

Success Secret #1 – Have the Courage to Fail in Order to Succeed

To be extremely successful, you must have great courage and be willing to take risks. This is the single secret every one of the Fearless Leaders in this book was either great at or had mastered.

Success Secret #2 – Get Comfortable Being Uncomfortable

With this secret you were introduced to the peak performance graph. You learned to identify your secret fears, identify and resolve fear of success, fear of rejection and fear of selling. You learned powerful techniques to resolve fear including accepting and coming to peace with the worst-case scenario. You also learned several techniques to increase your ability to be comfortable with discomfort.

Success Secret #3 – Own It: No Blaming Complaining or Excuses

The amazing leader you read about with this secret was Nobel Peace Prize winner Leymah Gbowee, who, leading a group of seven other women, found a way to end Liberia's tragic 14-year long civil war. She made no excuses and initiated the conflict's peaceful resolution. For this secret you learned the three-steps to the "Own It" technique.

Success Secret #4 – Show Up Ready!

There were two sections devoted to this success secret. One focused on getting your conscious and subconscious minds aligned so that you are free of conflicting or subconscious blocks to achieving your goals. The second was on extraordinary preparation using a T3 attitude: technical, tactical and temperamental readiness.

Success Secret #5 – Be a Master of Mind Control

This secret is how to perform your best during your most important situations; the moments in your life where you can become great. Being a master of mind control is learning to stay in the present with your thoughts, emotions and actions, even under great duress. You learned the amazingly powerful, yet simple set/reset thought replacement technique to stay positive and present in your thinking. You also learned three levels of mental rehearsal.

Success Secret #6 – Value Critical Review

Critical review of your experiences is your greatest learning opportunity. Athletes, special forces military personnel and performers in general use critical reviews really well. You can too. Prepare to be your best, learn to stay present in the moment no matter what and then use review to learn how to be even better. Mastering this secret allows you to turn your setbacks into opportunities and big wins. A powerful technique you learned for this is Rewind/Review/Take2.

Success Secret #7 – Think with Mindfulness

Mindfulness has four parts: 1) Pay attention on purpose; 2) Be in the present moment ; 3) Stay non-judgmental; 4) Have absolute focus. We believe developing more mindful leaders especially in business and government is a needed evolutionary step. You can practice mindfulness anywhere doing anything.

Success Secret #8 – Create Mindful Moments

The mindful moment is the instant that allows you to be absolutely and fully present in your most powerful, creative, knowledgeable and wise self. You can create mindful moments that consciously take you off of auto-response and onto the opportunity for higher consciousness thinking.You learned about the importance of developing and strengthening your observer-self to break free of the unconscious auto-response cycle and use more free will.

Success Secret #9 – Mindfulness is Powerful

Mindfulness is a powerful thinking process for new solutions, creativity and understanding the ripple effect of decisions. The greater the frequency of your mindful moments, and the greater the length and depth of these moments, the more powerfully effective your mindfulness is. You also learned to use mindfulness during a disagreement.

Success Secret #10 – Climb the Consciousness Mountain

There are infinite levels of conscious awareness when we are being still in the mindful moment. Which level of consciousness you choose is up to you. Since what you do affects the lives of other people, it's vital you have great decision-making processes that allow you to be mindful and make higher conscious choices.

Success Secret #11 – Passion is the Fuel of Greatness

You learned one of the distinguishing traits of high-performance organizations is a focus on the one thing they are passionate about. You learned that leaders with unrelenting fire are often disruptors and that you need to identify your one thing to focus your passion on. This chapter presented you with a five-step technique you can use to find your passion. Nobody can tell you what your passion is, but once you have found it, you will be inspired to take action.

Success Secret #12 – The Impossible is Possible

When you combine mindful moments with your unrelenting fire sometimes what seemed impossible becomes possible. You read about the two-week turnaround of a professional sports team and how Jerry and Monique Sternin used positive deviants to save starving children in Viet Nam.

Cathy and "The Creed Seed"

The following parable was sent to me by a friend. Although I rewrote it to a fair extent, the basic premise remains unchanged. My research indicates that the original author is unknown, but please let me know if you find the origin of this story so I can give proper acknowledgment:

A successful CEO was growing old and knew it was time to choose a successor to take over his company. Instead of selecting one of his senior executives or board members, he deployed an unusual succession plan.

He gathered his young executives and announced, "It is time for me to step down and choose the next CEO. I have decided to choose one of you." The old man ignored their surprised responses and continued, "I am going to give each one of you a seed—a very special seed. I want you to plant the seed, water it regularly and return three months from today with the plant you have grown. I will then judge your results and choose the next CEO."

Jim, one of the young executives, went home and excitedly described to his wife his role in the unconventional succession plan. That evening, they went to a nursery and purchased a large pot, expensive, high-quality soil and organic fertilizer.

After about two weeks, some of the other executives began to talk about their plants, which were beginning to grow. Jim kept checking his seed, but it had not yet germinated. Three weeks, four weeks, five weeks went by and still nothing sprouted. By now, Jim's peers often spoke about their thriving plants, but Jim's seed still showed no signs of life.

Two months went by and Jim's soil remained barren. He did not confide his failure to his colleagues, who continued to boast about the growth of their seeds. But despite his disappointment, Jim continued to diligently water his seed.

Three months finally passed. On the morning of the dreaded inspection, Jim lay in bed and told his wife that he would rather submit his resignation than be subjected to the anticipated humiliation. Although she shared his frustration and disappointment, she encouraged him to attend the meeting and live up to his obligation to reconvene with the CEO. Jim was sick at the thought of the embarrassment he was about to face, but he knew that his wife was right.

When Jim entered the company's board room, he was amazed at the variety of lush and bountiful plants grown by the other junior executives. Apparently, no one else had killed their seed. Jim clutched his lifeless pot to his chest while doing his best to avoid eye contact with his colleagues, some of whom smirked, while others offered looks of sympathy.

When the CEO arrived, he surveyed the room and greeted the young executives, "My, what great plants, trees and flowers you have grown." The CEO spotted Jim through the foliage, holding his empty pot. He pointed and called Jim to join him at the front of the room. Jim was horrified. He thought, *the CEO sees that I'm a failure and plans to make an example of me. I just hope he does not fire me in front of everyone.*

Jim stood before the CEO, who asked him, "What happened to your seed?" Jim explained how he purchased quality soil and fertilizer and meticulously watered his seed during the entire three-month period.

When Jim was finished, the CEO turned to the crowd and announced, "Behold, your next Chief Executive Officer."

Jim could not believe his ears. He could not even grow a seed. How could he be expected to grow and nurture a company?

Then the CEO said, "Three months ago, I gave everyone in this room a seed. I told you to take the seed, plant it, water it and bring it back to me today. The seeds I gave you had been boiled and thus were incapable of germinating.

"When most of you found that your seeds would not grow, you substituted another seed for the one I gave you. Jim was the only person among your ranks with the courage and honesty to bring back the original seed. Therefore, I am appointing him to be our new CEO and each of you must immediately begin seeking employment elsewhere."

Clear and deliberate integrity will help you define which seeds to plant in order to achieve your aspirational values, desires, purposes and talents. From these seeds, you will reap your rewards.

Plant courage – reap confidence
Plant resilience – reap wellbeing
Plant consciousness – reap intention
Plant mindfulness – reap success

SELF-REFLECTION EXERCISES

Higher scores indicate more Fearless Leader traits.

Self-Reflection – Have the Courage to Fail in Order to Succeed
Score yourself on each question on a 1 to 5 scale in which:
1 = never/almost never
2 = seldom
3 = sometimes
4 = often
5 = almost always/always

1. When faced with an enormous opportunity that's also a risky challenge in which you could fail, do you take the opportunity?___
2. When you look at new opportunities, is your focus more on the potential than on the risks?___
3. Do you believe enough in your abilities to put your job or business on the line at times?___
4. Do you get excited about the lessons you learned when you fail and immediately make changes?___
5. Do others consider you someone who is willing to take risks?___

Self-Reflection – Get Comfortable Being Uncomfortable
Score yourself on each question on a 1 to 5 scale in which:
1 = never/almost never
2 = seldom
3 = sometimes
4 = often
5 = almost always/always

1. When choosing between a project you can do with ease and one that will force you to learn, grow and change, you choose the second one. __

2. You readily admit your mistakes.__

3. In your personal life you look for opportunities, even great opportunities to challenge yourself so you learn, grow and change.__

4. If you are physically active, you like pushing yourself hard enough to experience physical discomfort during your workouts.__

5. You welcome change.__

Self-Reflection – Own It! No Blaming Complaining or Excuses
Score yourself on each question on a 1 to 5 scale in which:
1 = never/almost never
2 = seldom
3 = sometimes
4 = often
5 = almost always/always

1. Do the people with whom you spend the most time take full responsibility for everything in their lives and not blame, complain or make excuses? __

2. When something goes wrong in your life, do you take full responsibility and not look for who or what to blame? __

3. Do you live each day in gratitude? __

4. You see mistakes as learning opportunities? __

5. When things go badly, you don't make excuses. __

Self-Reflection – Aligned Minds
Score yourself on each question on a 1 to 5 scale in which:
1 = never/almost never
2 = seldom
3 = sometimes
4 = often
5 = almost always/always

1. For my most important goals, I'm unstoppable. __
2. I look internally to identify goals that may conflict with other goals I'm committed to. For example, spending extra time at work and getting physically fit. __
3. I am aware when I have thoughts or feelings that indicate I'm not 100 percent committed to a goal. __
4. I notice the ease, the flow of energy when I'm completely aligned and committed to what I am focused on. __
5. Other people notice that I get into a flow and accomplish what I set out to do.__

Self-Reflection – Extraordinary Preparation
Score yourself on each question on a 1 to 5 scale in which:
1 = never/almost never
2 = seldom
3 = sometimes
4 = often
5 = almost always/always

1. I know the thoughts and emotions that help me be my best in the most important situations.__
2. I consciously create the emotions that will allow me to be my best, like courage, confidence and/or relaxation before engaging in challenging situations.__
3. I can increase or decrease my emotional or physical energy as I need to in different situations.__
4. I use a well-developed routine to get me in a state of mind to be my best.__
5. I value and create great starts.__

Self-Reflection – Be a Master of Mind Control
Score yourself on each question below on a 1 to 5 scale in which:
1 = never/almost never
2 = seldom
3 = sometimes

4 = often
5 = almost always/always

1.You are aware when you have destructive, negative or fearful thoughts.__
2. During your greatest challenges, under the highest stress, your thoughts and emotions help you be your best.__
3. When you have nervous or stress symptoms, you observe your own thinking to understand how you are creating the emotions with your thoughts.__
4. Your mind is very disciplined and you stay focused on what's important.__
5. When you have a destructive, negative or fearful thought you actively replace it with a thought that gives you a positive focus.__

Self-Reflection – Value Critical Review
Score yourself on each question on a 1 to 5 scale in which:
1 = never/almost never
2 = seldom
3 = sometimes
4 = often
5 = almost always/always

1. After all of your important moments, events, projects, or challenges, how often do you review successes and setbacks in microscopic detail and then make changes to improve as you go forward?__
2. If you are on a team of any kind, how often does your team review their successes and setbacks in great detail?__
3. If you review your setbacks in order to learn from them, how often do you go back and evaluate the assumptions you made that led to the setbacks?__
4. If you review your important events, do you then replay them over and over in your mind, doing them as optimally as you can imagine to retrain your brain and accelerate your success?__
5. You use your mistakes and setbacks to accelerate your success.__

Self-Reflection – Think with Mindfulness

Score yourself on each question on a 1 to 5 scale in which:

1 = never/almost never

2 = seldom

3 = sometimes

4 = often

5 = almost always/always

1. Other people notice you can be extraordinarily, intentionally present with them.__

2. When taking on a challenge, you can enter that part of your mind where there is plenty of time and space to allow you to create innovative solutions.__

3. When an intelligent person presents a thought or a solution that is either different or even opposite from yours, you can listen without judgment and consider their point of view.__

4. You practice on a regular basis strengthening your ability to be nonjudgmental about potential solutions to difficult challenges.__

5. You consciously and regularly practice slowing down your thoughts, your breathing and your heart rate.__

Self-Reflection - Create Mindful Moments

Score yourself on each question on a 1 to 5 scale in which:

1 = never/almost never

2 = seldom

3 = sometimes

4 = often

5 = almost always/always

1. Do you consciously enhance your awareness when you are seeking a creative solution?__

2. Do you recognize when your mind is on auto-response and shouldn't be?__

3. Do you consciously pay attention to and strengthen your observer-self?__

4. In a disagreement, can you remain calm?__

5. Do you intentionally create mindfulness in the moments when you most need it?__

Self-Reflection – Mindfulness is Powerful

Score yourself on each question on a 1 to 5 scale in which:

1 = never/almost never

2 = seldom

3 = sometimes

4 = often

5 = almost always/always

1. If asked, people who know you the best would say you exercise excellent willpower in your personal life.__

2. As a leader, you have the will to focus on long-term success even at the expense of short-term success.__

3. When faced with a difficult challenge, you pay attention to what you're thinking and feeling.__

4. When it's most important, you expand the depth and time of your mindful moments.__

5. During your mindful moments, you create more options, including higher consciousness alternatives to solve your important challenges.__

Self-Reflection – Climb the Consciousness Mountain

Score yourself on each question on a 1 to 5 scale in which:

1 = never/almost never

2 = seldom

3 = sometimes

4 = often

5 = almost always/always

1. You recognize different choices that range from completely self-serving to benefiting all.__

2. When faced with what appears to be an either or decision, you find creative answers to make it an "and" solution. For example, a product can be either higher quality or lower price. You pursue a solution that is both higher quality and lower price.__

3. You understand that you are your only real competition and focus on competing with yourself, not with others.__

4. You apply a decision-making process you trust to make your most important decisions.__

5. Your decisions and actions reflect the greater good of all.__

Self-Reflection – Passion is the Fuel of Greatness
Score yourself on each question on a 1 to 5 scale in which:
1 = never/almost never
2 = seldom
3 = sometimes
4 = often
5 = almost always/always

1. I know the one thing that I am most passionate about and am engaged with.__

2. Others comment on how happy and/or passionate I am about my work.__

3. My decisions are based at least in part on my passions.__

4. My goals are aligned with my passions.__

5. My days are filled with doing what I love with people I enjoy.__

Self-Reflection – The Impossible is Possible
Score yourself on each question on a 1 to 5 scale in which:
1 = never/almost never
2 = seldom
3 = sometimes
4 = often
5 = almost always/always

1. When you are told something you want to do "can't be done," you believe you can find a way to do it.___
2. When something important to you initially seems like it might be impossible, you get excited to find a solution.___
3. You create mindful moments to help you achieve what you are passionate about.___
4. The bigger the challenge, the more excited you are to take it on.___
5. You find solutions to challenges when others can't.___

15709819R10095

Made in the USA
San Bernardino, CA
04 October 2014